THE DIESEL THAT DID IT

RAILROADS PAST & PRESENT

H. ROGER GRANT AND THOMAS HOBACK, EDITORS

Recent titles in the Railroads Past and Present series

The Station Agent and the American Railroad Experience
H. Roger Grant

Crossroads of a Continent
Peter A. Hansen, Don L. Hofsommer, and
Carlos Arnaldo Schwantes

Narrow Gauge in the Tropics
Augustus J. Veenendaal Jr.

Amtrak, America's Railroad
Geoffrey H. Doughty, Jeffrey T. Darbee, and Eugene Harmon

The Panama Railroad
Peter Pyne

Last Train to Texas
Fred W. Frailey

Transportation and the American People
H. Roger Grant

American Steam Locomotives
William L. Withuhn

My Life with Trains
Jim McClellan

The Railroad Photography of Lucius Beebe and Charles Clegg
Tony Reevy

Chicago Union Station
Fred Ash

John W. Barriger III
H. Roger Grant

Riding the Rails
Robert D. Krebs

Wallace W. Abbey
Kevin P. Keefe and Scott Lothes

Branch Line Empires
Michael Bezilla with Luther Gette

Indianapolis Union and Belt Railroads
Jeffrey Darbee

Railroads and the American People
H. Roger Grant

Derailed by Bankruptcy
Howard H. Lewis

Electric Interurbans and the American People
H. Roger Grant

The Iron Road in the Prairie State
Simon Cordery

The Lake Shore Electric Railway Story
Herbert H. Harwood Jr. and Robert S. Korach

The Railroad That Never Was
Herbert H. Harwood Jr.

James J. Hill's Legacy to Railway Operations
Earl J. Currie

Railroaders without Borders
H. Roger Grant

The Iowa Route
Don L. Hofsommer

The Railroad Photography of Jack Delano
Tony Reevy

INDIANA UNIVERSITY PRESS

Facing, Santa Fe's gleaming new diesel-electric FT is flanked by two examples of the railroad's ultimate steam locomotives, 4-8-4 No. 2908 (left) and 2-10-4 No. 5006, at Clovis, New Mexico, 1944. Trains *magazine, Kalmbach Media*

THE DIESEL THAT DID IT
GENERAL MOTORS' FT LOCOMOTIVE

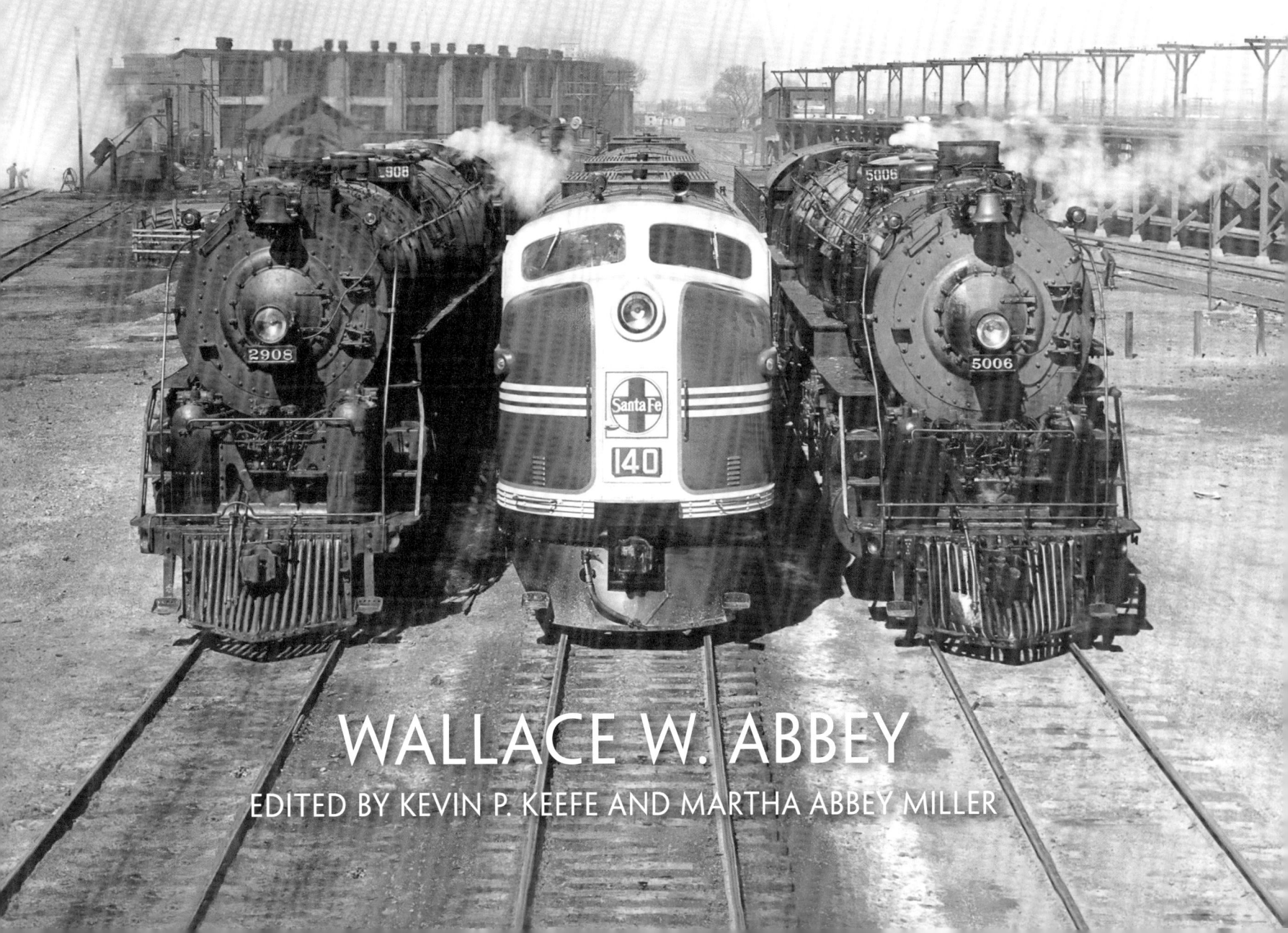

WALLACE W. ABBEY
EDITED BY KEVIN P. KEEFE AND MARTHA ABBEY MILLER

This book is a publication of

Indiana University Press
Office of Scholarly Publishing
Herman B Wells Library 350
1320 East 10th Street
Bloomington, Indiana 47405 USA

iupress.org

© 2022 by Martha Abbey Miller

All rights reserved
No part of this book may be reproduced or utilized in any form or by any means, electronic or mechanical, including photocopying and recording, or by any information storage and retrieval system, without permission in writing from the publisher. The paper used in this publication meets the minimum requirements of the American National Standard for Information Sciences—Permanence of Paper for Printed Library Materials, ANSI Z39.48-1992.

Manufactured in the United States of America

First printing 2022

Cataloging information is available from the Library of Congress.

ISBN 978-0-253-06278-9 (hardback)
ISBN 978-0-253-06280-2 (ebook)

Contents

Foreword vii
Acknowledgments ix

1. Ride with the Ghost of the Santa Fe: *The Legacy of the Atchison, Topeka and Santa Fe*   3

2. Too Many Santa Fes!: *Overview of the Railroad That Introduced the FT*   17

3. Mechanical Motion, Set to Music: *Santa Fe Steam at the Dawn of the FT*   35

4. Hamilton, Winton, Kettering: *The Evolution of Electro-Motive*   51

5. Finally, a Locomotive Prime Mover: *The Birth of the Legendary 567 Engine*   65

6. The Model F Standard: *In the End, Electro-Motive Had to Prove It Could Handle Freight*   77

7. A Mikado on the Prairies, a Mallet in the Mountains: *The 103 Goes to Work on the Santa Fe Trail*   99

8. Lessons Learned from the 103: *What the 103 Did, and Did Not Do, on the Santa Fe*   113

9. A Big Coming-out Party: *Santa Fe Rolls Out Its First Freight Diesel*   121

10. Electro-Motive Goes to War: *A Locomotive Builder Serves the US Navy*   143

11. The Unions and the Laws: *The Challenges to Operating Efficiency*   153

12. Eighty Locomotives the Hard Way: *Building the Fleet One EMD Order at a Time*   167

13. A Class by Itself: *The Author's Retrospective*   187

Bibliography   205
Index   207

FOREWORD

"The diesel that did it."

Trains magazine editor David P. Morgan did not assign the attribute lightly when he chose the title for his tribute to the Electro-Motive FT in the February 1960 issue. "Suppose you were asked this question," Morgan wrote:

> What single locomotive constructed since 1900 has had the greatest impact upon U.S. railroading? Surely your answer would have to be Electro-Motive No. 103, the 193-foot, 900,000-pound, 5,400-horsepower machine spread across these pages. When the 103 eased through the gates of her La Grange birthplace in November 1939, diesel-electric road freight motive power was only a theory, and by her builder's own admission this dark green, yellow-striped locomotive was an experiment. Eleven months and 83,764 miles later, steam's century-old grip on the freight train had been permanently broken and No. 103 was the prototype for the world's first standardized, mass-produced line of diesel freight locomotives. There is no equal in the annals of railroading for such a swift closing of the gap between fancy and fact.

Wally Abbey got it, right from his earliest encounters with Electro-Motive Division's "Model F." A camera-toting high school student with a fascination for railroading, Abbey and a few like-minded friends from Evanston Township High School north of Chicago sought out and photographed Santa Fe 100-class FTs still fresh from La Grange in the mid-1940s. Abbey knew firsthand and appreciated the magnificence of steam but sensed the significance and revolutionary implications of the FT.

Facing, The author at work on his college summer job as a Chicago-area tower operator for the Chicago & North Western. *Wallace W. Abbey Collection*

Growing up in Evanston, Illinois, Abbey's love of railroading manifested itself early, watching Chicago & North Western (C&NW) trains in his hometown, and those of Frisco and Santa Fe while visiting his grandparents in Cherryvale, Kansas, in the years leading up to World War II. He took his first railroad photograph, an image of C&NW's *Peninsula 400*, in 1940 at age 13, and thanks to friendship with hometown crews at the C&NW yard in South Evanston (where suburban trains laid up overnight), he learned to operate a locomotive before he could drive a car. Summer jobs, first as a diesel repairman's helper at Santa Fe's 21st Street diesel shop in Chicago in 1944 and then as an operator/leverman at C&NW towers in the Chicago area, set the stage for a career in railroading.

Although he gave serious consideration to working as a musician, Abbey followed his father's lead and in 1945 enrolled in journalism studies at the University of Kansas at Lawrence. Not surprisingly, he parlayed that degree into an impressive career in the railroad industry as a journalist, public-relations man, and rail consultant. Between July 1950 and early 1954, Abbey served as associate editor at *Trains* magazine, followed by work with the Association of Western Railways (1954–1956) and *Railway Age* (1956–1959). In 1959, he joined the public-relations department at the Soo Line, where he remained until 1970. After a stint as an independent rail consultant, he moved to public relations with the Milwaukee Road from 1975 until 1980, followed by Trailer Train (1980–1982), and finally the Transportation Technology Center in Pueblo, Colorado, from 1982 until 1991.

Informed by nearly five decades as a professional railroader, the genesis of this book can be directly traced to the 21st Street diesel shop in the spring of 1945 and Abbey's encounter with Santa Fe's No. 167, an A-B-B-A FT set geared for 90 miles per hour, outfitted with steam generators for passenger service, and assigned to the railway's premier Chicago–Los Angeles *Super Chief*. Abbey's investigations revealed that in addition to the 167, 10 more FT sets would be equipped with steam generators and high-speed gearing, and temporarily reassigned to passenger service. Furthermore, five A-B-B-A FT sets, Nos. 100–104, had been transferred to Kansas City–Chicago manifest freight service.

"That fact-finding mission," Abbey notes, "changed the pattern of my explorations of Chicago's railroads. I began to concentrate on those Santa Fe diesels for the balance of my high school days."

Santa Fe picked up the first production Model FTs—two 5,400-horsepower A-B-B-A sets ordered in September 1940, even before Electro-Motive demonstrator 103 completed its historic 83,764-mile barnstorming tour—and purchased the most. Delivery of two four-unit sets numbered 178 and 179 in August 1945 gave Santa Fe a total of 320 FTs.

From his unexpected encounter with Nos. 101 and 167 on a gloomy 1944 afternoon in McCook, Illinois, to workaday views of dress-blue A-B-B-As of FTs—at Joliet, Illinois; and Turner, Holliday, and Zarah, Kansas; on the curves of Olathe Hill in the Mill Creek Valley; and from the tower at Ottawa Junction, Kansas—Abbey, one of the most respected photographers of our time, documented Santa Fe's FTs in their prime.

Some 60 years later, he crafted *The Diesel That Did It* with the same enthusiasm he afforded the brand-new FTs at the 21st Street diesel shop. This work stands in tribute to the remarkable machine that changed railroading and to the man moved to celebrate it: Wallace W. Abbey.

Greg J. McDonnell

Greg J. McDonnell is a veteran railroad writer and editor of Kalmbach's annual publication *Locomotive*.

ACKNOWLEDGMENTS

"Wait until your father gets home from the office."

My sister, Maggie, and I would, when we were young, occasionally misbehave badly enough to warrant our mother's need for reinforcement. At dinnertime, Dad would arrive from his day at the Soo Line Railroad in downtown Minneapolis to learn of his daughters' exploits. Mom, for whom I was named Martha, would say in exasperation, "Wally, speak to your girls."

"Hello, girls!"

Wally Abbey, who passed away in 2014, was a great father, if not a strict disciplinarian.

He was also a great railroader. Wally's love for trains, especially locomotives, and his knowledge of railroad operations were ideal subject matter for his skills as a writer and a photographer. His journalism studies at the University of Kansas led him to a rich career at *Trains*; Association of Western Railroads; *Railway Age*; the Soo Line; the Milwaukee Road; Trailer Train; and the Transportation Technology Center in Pueblo, Colorado, where he and Mom retired. Along the way, Wally formed a consulting company and a publishing company. At the latter, in 1984, he self-published *The Little Jewel: Soo Line Railroad and the locomotives that make it go*.

For years, Wally poured time and energy into his FT story, grateful to Indiana University (IU) Press for agreeing to publish it. Sadly, illness crept up, forcing him to set the project aside. I know Wally would have wanted to thank those who helped him do his primary research, at Atchison, Topeka and Santa Fe Railway; Barriger National Railroad Library; California State

Railroad Museum; DeGolyer Library; The Denver Public Library; Electro-Motive Division and elsewhere within General Motors Corporation; Kalmbach Publishing Co.; Kansas Historical Society; Library of Congress; Minnesota Historical Society; and other locations.

Wally would have thanked by name those who helped make this book possible, no doubt displaying his wry wit as he did so. Many are listed in the bibliography. Others were everyday railroaders up and down the line who were to Wally a source of delight. He also would have thanked his career colleagues and his family, especially his wife, Martha, who predeceased him, for her partnership both at home and on research expeditions. Certainly, Wally's high school railfan buddies—Chic Kerrigan, Dave Wallace, and the late Tom Harley—would warrant a special nod. Among those who provided feedback on manuscript drafts were Larry Brashear, Fred W. Frailey, the late John Gruber, Nick Modders, and Joe Swanson. Had Wally written these acknowledgments himself, many other names would be included. To each of you, thank you.

I add my own sincere appreciation for Kevin P. Keefe, without whom this book could not have been published. An enthusiastic coeditor, Kevin contributed richly to each aspect of Wally's story: its narrative, its photos and captions, and its production. Kevin reached out to Indiana University Press, to whom we express grateful thanks for putting Wally's book back on its schedule. It's been a pleasure to work with Dave Hulsey, Anna Francis, Darja Malcolm-Clarke, Stephen Williams, and their teams—a different crew than was assisting Wally 20 years ago, but with the same professionalism and zeal.

In 2018, Kevin, Scott Lothes, and IU Press collaborated on *Wallace W. Abbey: A Life in Railroad Photography*. Readers and railfans will enjoy this look at Wally's railroading career through the lens of his camera. The entire collection of Wally's images, 30,000, has since 2010 been in the care of the Center for Railroad Photography & Art, of which Scott is president and executive director. A hearty thanks goes to Scott and his team for their support.

Kevin, who is on the center's board of directors, took great care in selecting the images for *The Diesel That Did It*. I find deep joy that the cover photograph, featuring No. 101 with Wally standing nearby in a plaid jacket, was taken by Chic Kerrigan, his high school friend. I offer my thanks to Al Chione, the photo's copyright owner. Al and Chic are but two of the team members whom Kevin assembled to complete Wally's book, in his honor.

Many thanks to Greg McDonnell for his generous foreword, which gets the book off to a terrific start and reminds us to share the FT spotlight with Wally's boss and friend, David P. Morgan.

We appreciate Robert S. McGonigal, retired editor of *Classic Trains* magazine and manager of Kalmbach's media library, for his extensive help in image selection. Michael Iden, retired motive-power chief for the Union Pacific, offered invaluable technical expertise. Author Fred W. Frailey, a longtime *Trains* columnist and longtime supporter of this FT story, also provided a valuable critique. Dave Styffe used his extensive knowledge of the Santa Fe routes to create the fine map on the end covers, to which readers will frequently refer.

Photographer Stan Kistler generously contributed several outstanding photos. Obtaining permissions for other photographs took a bit of effort, given the passage of time. We apologize for any lapse along the way. The curators and archivists with whom Kevin and I spoke, including Shelby Bader of Kettering University Archives, were universally delighted to help bring this FT story to the public eye. We thank the copyright holders and are pleased to have been able to include the breadth of images that appear in this book.

In Wally's absence, and on behalf of my sister, Maggie, and the Abbey family, Kevin and I are grateful to you all.

Martha Abbey Miller
Prescott, Arizona

THE DIESEL THAT DID IT

ONE RIDE WITH THE GHOST OF THE SANTA FE

The Legacy of the Atchison, Topeka and Santa Fe

THIS BOOK BRINGS TO LIFE WHAT WE SHOULD REMEMBER AS the Atchison, Topeka and Santa Fe Railway: about how, beginning in the days when diesel engines, electrical power transmissions, and locomotives were learning to get along with each other more or less politely, the Santa Fe became the first among American railroads to diligently apply diesel-electric motive power to the task of moving freight trains along its main lines. We want to see what those freight diesels did for the railroads, especially for the Santa Fe.

This book is also about the type of diesel-electric the Santa Fe used in its mainline road freight train service, the Model F of General Motors Corporation. The locomotives were also known as FTs; the *F* signified Freight. And the *T*? Many railroaders believe it stood for Thirteen, which as we'll see was a significant number in terms of horsepower. The Santa Fe assigned its FTs both the class and road-number series 100.

In their day, the FTs were a mighty advancement in locomotive art. Today we'd regard them as primitive, and from where we sit now, we'd be right. But we wouldn't have called them primitive in the years just before and during World War II. Then, they were the newest and fanciest kids on the block. The Model F changed the course of railroading for the better and for all time. Together,

---

Facing, Passenger diesel 14 rides the turntable at Santa Fe's 18th Street diesel facility in Chicago. In the background, dining car 1192 is parked at the Fred Harvey commissary platform. *Photo Santa Fe Railway,* Trains *magazine, Kalmbach Media*

the Santa Fe and its first freight diesel-electrics introduced an operational renaissance the railroad industry had long needed. They did so in remarkably difficult times. The renaissance might not have happened had the times not been so strenuous. It could have happened more rapidly, and doubtless would have, had the nation not been at war.

Here, we'll get to know the designer and manufacturer of Santa Fe's FTs, the outfit we've known down through time as the Electro-Motive Corporation, or the Electro-Motive Division of General Motors, or just plain Electro-Motive, or EMC, or most often EMD. The company is no longer a member of the General Motors family; today it's called Electro-Motive Diesel, a brand of Progress Rail, a Caterpillar subsidiary. For years, EMD supplied most of the diesel-electrics for the railroad industry. Ultimately, two dozen railroads would acquire the FT.

Famous in its day—among locomotive fanciers, anyway—the FT probably is forgotten now except by the fatally dedicated. No one at today's EMD nor on today's railroads was around that far back in history. Were the FT somehow to come back, it wouldn't fit the patterns and practices of contemporary Santa Fe operations. Nor would it fit anywhere else.

The FT won't come back, of course, although even at this writing it's not altogether gone. The car body of one section of the first FT built has been in a museum in St. Louis since 1961. It's memorialized as a national historical engineering landmark. Another unit that belonged originally to the Northern Pacific may still be around in Mexico.

The Atchison, Topeka and Santa Fe Railway is anything but forgotten. What was long known simply as the Santa Fe, and then became part of the Burlington Northern Santa Fe, remains readily identifiable by tradition. The manner in which the former Santa Fe serves the nation's commerce has changed greatly over the years, as one might expect—and hope. After all, our story begins a long time ago.

We will look at freight dieselization from many vantage points, observing how, simultaneously, the FT was regarded as an engineering marvel, a balance sheet boon, an operational challenge, an employee threat, a wartime workhorse, and a new battleground for the labor unions.

To tell our tale, perspective will be as important as will be fact. In pursuit of perspective and fact both, we must go see the Santa Fe as it was at the time the 100s were about to come on the scene.

How the Passenger Traffic and Operating Departments have managed what we're about to experience is not for us to question. They probably wouldn't tell us if they knew, and quite likely they haven't got a clue! However the ghost of the Santa Fe long past has managed it . . .

It's the waning summer of 1939.

It's Tuesday.

We're in Chicago.

We're entering a large brick, terra cotta, and brownstone building that stands where Dearborn Street meets Polk, a block off State. The clock in the ornate tower advises that the evening hours are approaching. Yellow and Checker taxicabs and Parmelee Transfer limousines swarm around the entrance. People with their luggage and in their traveling clothes are everywhere. We're excited by the anticipation, the sounds, the smells, the grit. We're taking the train to California!

Inside, beyond waiting rooms and the newsstand, under the dark canopy that arches over the tracks, we see Pullman sleepers, coaches, diners, steam locomotives, stiff-capped conductors, and red-capped baggage attendants. Trains of the Chicago & Eastern Illinois, Chicago & Western Indiana, Erie, Grand Trunk Western, Monon, Wabash, and Santa Fe are moving in and out. This is a busy place.

Welcome to Dearborn Station!

One train stands out from the others. Its cars shine in bright contrast to the darker trains around it. A backlit royal-purple sign beneath the windows in the rounded end of its last car announces that this is the *Super Chief* of the Santa Fe, the train that's going to take us to Los Angeles.

If you'll just show your ticket to the gateman, we'll move out onto the wooden platform. From there we'll step up into the luxury of this remarkable conveyance.

In three years, the *Super Chief* has become a metaphor for the Santa Fe of the future, even for a distant and hard-to-imagine future in which there might be few intercity passenger trains in America.

Fashioned in fluted stainless steel, air-conditioned, and steam heated, the train lavishly serves a hundred travelers, offering sleeping accommodations of several sorts, tavern lounges, a marvelous rolling restaurant, and a barber shop staffed by a valet and a manicurist—well worth the extra fare of $15 (1939). The *Super Chief* is the most pampered train on the Santa Fe. It's designed for the most pampered of clientele.

In large part for the *Super Chief*, for the nearly as upscale *Chief*, and for *El Capitan*, an extra-fare all-chair-car companion to the *Super Chief*, the Santa Fe is rethinking and reshaping the main lines of its railroad. Much of this work on the grade, alignment, and quality of the track will make life easier for the freight diesels, too, when they come.

Today and today only our *Super Chief* will be capable of magic. When we slip out of Dearborn Station promptly at 7:15 p.m., we'll emerge into full daylight. We'll travel from Chicago to Los Angeles in 39 hours, 45 minutes before the sun goes down. From our private bedroom, or from our table in that superb rolling restaurant with its excellent Fred Harvey service, or from our easy chair amid the striking southwest ambiance of the observation lounge in the car called *Navajo*, we'll avail ourselves of an opportunity never before granted and never granted since: to inspect the entire main line of the Santa Fe to California in the fullness of both daylight and history.

Furthermore—and we'd like to see the look on the face of the vice president of operations when he hears about this!—for

QUINTESSENTIAL RAILROAD MAN

Edward Ripley. *Photo Santa Fe Railway, Trains magazine, Kalmbach Media*

Born in Dorchester, Massachusetts, in 1845, Edward Ripley was as American as they come. His family, colonists, had settled in the mid-1600s. After attending public schools, Ripley took a job as a dry goods merchant in Boston. Six years later, he joined the Pennsylvania Railroad as a freight agent, discovering his career of choice. He worked up through the ranks of the Chicago, Burlington & Quincy and the Milwaukee Road.

The 1890s were turbulent for the Atchison, Topeka and Santa Fe. Various financial scandals threw the railroad into bankruptcy. When it emerged from receivership in 1895, Edward Ripley became Santa Fe's 14th president. He had his work cut out for him.

Certainly, public opinion of the railroad was not high. But this was not Ripley's only challenge. Like other railroads, the Santa Fe had moved quickly across the prairie in its haste to claim western territory, lay down tracks, and build bridges. Its workmanship—stone and steel, rails and ties—was high quality, but there resulted still a sort of disorganized enthusiasm that needed to be tamed.

This, Edward Ripley did. He was a large man, wide shouldered and barrel chested. He looked like a railroad man, and with decades of experience up and down the line, he acted like one too. Over his presidency (1896–1920), Ripley continued the Santa Fe's trend toward corporate conservatism, eschewing large dividends to reinvest its earnings into improvements and expansion.

With raw energy, the railroads had moved more quickly than had the government. The West lacked highways; even many roads were unpaved. The Santa Fe route led its crew and passengers into rather remote places. To provide comfort and services, Ripley had added reading rooms at Santa Fe's terminal points. Here, train crews could shower, play billiards, and relax. Ripley was instrumental, too, in growing Santa Fe's partnership with Fred Harvey, whose restaurants were renowned along the Santa Fe for their hospitality and quality.

In 1917, during World War I, the government took control of America's railroads to avert a national strike. Ripley shared oversight of the Santa Fe with William Storey, the railway's federal manager. When Ripley retired from the Santa Fe on the first day of 1920 (before passing away a month later), Storey was elected president.

The towns of Ripley, California, and Ripley, Oklahoma, are a small part of the legacy of Edward Ripley. They remind us, 100 years later, of the contributions he made to building the railroads of the West.

The red, white, and purple of the *Super Chief*'s drumhead adorns the rear end of the observation car *Navajo*, photographed in Chicago in June 1937.
Photo Santa Fe Railway, Wallace W. Abbey Collection

The lead EA diesel of Santa Fe's *El Capitan* from California arrives next to the *Dixie Flagler* of the Chicago & Eastern Illinois, at Chicago's Dearborn Station. Trains *magazine, Kalmbach Media*

Above, Santa Fe's A1 No. 10 leads train 11, the *Kansas Cityan*, before departure from Dearborn Station in 1938. *Photo Warren Fancher,* Trains *magazine, Kalmbach Media*

Facing, Officials gawk at EMC's E6 demonstrator 822 at Chillicothe, Illinois, during a trip hauling the *Kansas Cityan* on October 22, 1937. *Photo Roland E. Collons Collection, DeGolyer Library, Southern Methodist University*

a fair part of our trip we'll travel simultaneously over two widely diverse routes. This we must do if we're to appreciate the scope and breadth of the Santa Fe, as well as its length.

Our magical *Super Chief* will transport us over its customary route, called the Northern District, across Illinois and Missouri; through central Kansas; across the southeast corner of Colorado; up over the storied passes of Raton and Glorieta in New Mexico to a crossing of the Rio Grande south of Albuquerque; across northwestern New Mexico, northern Arizona, and Southern California to the notch in the mountains called Cajon Pass; then down into the Los Angeles basin on the Pacific Ocean.

Shortly after we pass Emporia in Kansas, this magic trip will also veer more to the south and then to the west. We'll traverse the long and progressively more arid stretches and the not-inconsiderable obstacles of elevation that lie along what Santa Fe railroaders call the Southern District: down through south-central Kansas, across the Oklahoma and Texas panhandles, and into New Mexico well south and east of Raton. We'll go from the drainage of the Cottonwood River in Kansas to the valley of the Rio Grande in New Mexico. Then, climbing away west of Belen, we'll rejoin the Northern District within the limits of the interlocking plant at Dalies. There we'll merge seamlessly with our alternate self and proceed on to Los Angeles. Neat trick!

This Southern District is not renowned for its passenger boardings. There aren't that many sizable centers of population along the way compared to the number of cities of the Northern District; Amarillo is the most notable. The other premium and even most of the conventional transcontinental passenger and mail trains traverse much the same northern route over which the *Super Chief* is scheduled.

The southern route has its own job. It takes most transcontinental freight trains around the more citified Northern District.

Above, Seen through the windshield of the FT demonstrator diesel, a steam-powered freight approaches at the tiny depot in Aikman, Kansas. *Photo Santa Fe Railway, kansasmemory.org, Kansas Historical Society*

Facing, A 2-8-2 provides helper service for the E1 diesel on train 21, the *El Capitan*, Wootton, Colorado, on June 26, 1938. Note the diesel maintainer standing in the doorway. *Photo Otto C. Perry, Western History Collection, The Denver Public Library*

It relieves the Santa Fe of the arduous and expensive task of hoisting its freight business up one side of a couple of mountain ranges and then hanging onto it tightly ere it tumble down the other side. Long-haul freight certainly doesn't need Raton and Glorieta. Farther west, in Arizona and California, there are more than enough mountains.

Quite possibly, no railroad lavishes as much attention on a passenger train as the Santa Fe expends on its *Super Chief*. It's the freight trains, though, that really pay the bills, the employees, the bondholders, and the stockholders, and it's the freight trains that in large part make luxurious passenger trains like the *Super Chief* possible. It's the freight trains of the Southern District to which Electro-Motive's Model F largely will be dedicated.

To be sure, we'll find Model Fs in freight service elsewhere, and for a while some of them will even show up leading the *Super Chief*. But in the larger scheme of things, the Model Fs, which we'll know also as the FTs, will merely begin the process of dieselizing the Santa Fe's entire service, leaving the end of the process to their lineal descendants.

On this trip we'll see no ox-drawn prairie schooners on the Santa Fe Trail. Ours will be a journey through today—that is, through 1939—not through the days of westward expansion that preceded the Civil War. We'll be riding through history, to be sure, but we'll be visiting a time that credentialed retellers of railroads' past seem to regard as not historical enough—perhaps

not *early* enough?—to be worthy of study. To each his own, but stick with us and you'll see much highly significant railroad history being made.

Nor will we see mile-long trains of coal, or 70-mile-an-hour rail-borne convocations of highway trailers and containers on flat cars, or pallid attempts by something called Amtrak to emulate the train we're riding. We'll hear no conversations, read no literature, about turbochargers or computers or modular electronic control systems aboard diesel-electric locomotives.

The development of the diesel prime mover for railroad service, as pursued by Electro-Motive, is at the stage where a pair of helical aluminum blowers geared to the drive shaft can handle the heavy breathing. Modular electronic control systems and computers are yet to be invented for railroad use—for any use, for that matter. It will be nine years before Bell Labs introduces the transistor, the tiny component basic to all electronic marvels.

As a matter of fact, the diesel-electric locomotive is a mere infant. Our red-nosed ranger has few relatives on railroads anywhere around the country. Diesels in this summer of 1939 are powering a few premium passenger trains here and there and are shuffling cars in some of the yards of a handful of railroads, but it would be premature to claim these deviations as a trend. When its Model Fs begin to arrive, the Santa Fe will be the first American railroad to entrust to diesel-electric power portions of all three of its services: passenger, freight, and switching.

Facing, A pair of Santa Fe's giant 5000-class 2-10-4s teams up on an 86-car eastbound freight train east of Belen, New Mexico, on June 28, 1947. *Photo Otto C. Perry, Western History Collection, The Denver Public Library*

Above, The 1-spot passenger diesel of 1935 approaches the US 66 overpass east of Flagstaff, Arizona, with the westbound *Super Chief*. *Photo Santa Fe Railway, Wallace W. Abbey Collection*

Even so, even here on the Santa Fe in 1939, when one speaks of a locomotive, the modifier "steam" is most often a given. From a limited experience with diesels comes a limited acceptance of the idea of diesels. Why, *real* locomotives boil water to make steam! They use that steam to push pistons, which shove rods, which turn drive wheels! To move a train—a freight train, especially—is no job for a petroleum-fueled internal-combustion machine. Don't be surprised if veteran steam-locomotive handlers disparage the new diesels. Or if they tend to see them as toys. Or as something to actively resist.

Ahead, beyond the turn of the century, we'd have a tough time appreciating this Santa Fe of the late 1930s. But right now, we're *in* the late 1930s. Looking at what we see, we find it just as impossible to imagine what the Santa Fe will be like in the 2000s. Truly, the days of the FTs will be remarkable when they arrive, which will be soon. For our purposes here today, though, the time beyond the FTs is almost too far in the future to deal with.

Oh! We're moving! Didn't feel us start! Let's go back to the *Navajo*. Through those rear windows, and in the chapters ahead, we'll watch our Santa Fe of 1939 unfold. Got your timetable?

It's a relief to escape into the quiet and privacy of the *Super Chief*. The world outside, these United States included, is in economic and political turmoil. The wounds on the national body of a half-generation of economic depression are by no means healed. Nor are the wounds of concurrent years of drought that uprooted crops and farmers both, that saw arable Great Plains topsoil blow into the Atlantic Ocean.

But building the nation's capacity for manufacturing munitions is certainly expediting the national recovery. Europe and Asia are at war. For years our government has been involving us increasingly in the European conflict even as it's been asserting our neutrality. The United States is in fact arming the free world.

After World War I, we told ourselves we no longer needed a huge defense capability. We'd scrapped the one we had. About 15 months from now, President Franklin Roosevelt will want the United States to become what he'll call the great "arsenal of democracy." As he coins the phrase in a "fireside chat" over radio nationwide, the conversion of our heavy industry into a wartime manufactory of unprecedented size and scope will already be underway. Here in 1939, the intensifying military buildup is being felt in the Santa Fe's traffic levels and in its orders for new freight cars. The Santa Fe, too, is gearing up.

Facing, The dramatic chasm of Canyon Diablo, Arizona, is barely visible in this view of the approaching viaduct from the cab of a westbound freight. The San Francisco Peaks loom in the distance. *Photo Wallace W. Abbey,* Trains *magazine, Kalmbach Media*

An ancient 4-6-2 steam locomotive assists the E1 diesel on the eastbound *Chief* as it climbs through Sullivan's Curve on Cajon Pass. *Photo Santa Fe Railway, kansasmemory.org, Kansas Historical Society*

TWO TOO MANY SANTA FES!

Overview of the Railroad That Introduced the FT

SANTA FE DERIVES FROM THE SPANISH TERM FOR "HOLY faith." It's the name of an ancient settlement in the mountains of northern New Mexico to which commercial trade from the Missouri River began over a wagon trail in 1821.

It's fitting that our host for this trip here in 1939 should style itself as a latter-day "Trail of Holy Faith." We'll see in the Santa Fe a strong and inbred confidence in railroad transportation as a private enterprise; a confidence in the use of vehicles to carry people long distances on flanged wheels; a confidence in the long-term value of continually improving the railroad mode of movement, sometimes on a grand scale. The Santa Fe is an acknowledged innovator, yet it's a conservative industry leader. It's a consistent boon to its stockholders. It has helped the West grow and prosper. It has grown and prospered with the West.

The Santa Fe's most public face is a blend of Spanish architecture; Native American culture; travel to and through the American Southwest; sightseeing packages called Indian Detours; trackside hostelries and dining cars operated with the Fred Harvey expertise; and, recently, bright stainless-steel streamliners.

Railroading, though, isn't only catering to passengers and tourists, notwithstanding Santa Fe's principal advertising messages and the size of its passenger business. Railroading is a lot more about moving the raw products and finished goods that supply our national economy from wherever they come to wherever they need to go. Railroading blends the crafts of construction, communication, and transportation on a grand scale. You might not find a similar combination with such a big job to do anywhere else in American industry.

Being familiar with railroads, we know the characteristics that distinguish one from another tend to be superficial. Beneath their surfaces and behind their trademarks, advertising themes, and self-applied identities, all railroads are pretty much the same, though some are loath to admit it. Fundamentally, they use the same technologies. They vary greatly in length but, in a manner of speaking and with certain quaint exceptions, one is just as wide as the next.

All railroad companies use much the same types of rolling equipment. Generally, they face the same unions across bargaining tables to resolve the same differences concerning the use of manpower. They're governed by the same federal and state regulations. They buy their hardware mostly from the same relatively few vendors. The vendors, not the railroads themselves, do most of the research, development, and refinement of railroading's methods and machinery.

Railroads are both competitors and collaborators. Though they're mostly independent stockholder-owned entities, the common-carrier jobs they do jointly require them to delegate to industry-wide associations many of their important functions: publishing rates, setting mechanical standards, negotiating with labor unions, and trying to explain themselves to the public.

They share detailed manuals to ensure the interchangeability and reparability of their equipment anywhere in the national

CITADELS OF COMFORT IN THE DEVELOPING WEST

With an inbred penchant for quality, English-born Fred Harvey (1835–1901) emigrated to America as a teen, his parents in search of a better life. Working in a restaurant and then owning a café taught him to appreciate fresh ingredients and quality service. Over the years, yellow fever and typhoid, the hardships of the Civil War, and theft by his business partner of their café profits left Harvey undaunted. He bounced back, taking a job as a mail clerk for the Hannibal & St. Joseph Railroad in 1862. The nickname of the railroad, the Horrible and Slow Jolts, didn't deter the Chicago, Burlington & Quincy from acquiring it. Fred Harvey ascended in the Burlington's ranks, then added a second job, opening two more cafés.

Harvey often traveled by train, encountering the poor food, unsanitary lodging, and health risks that plagued every westbound rail traveler. Not only was Harvey's own health compromised by his earlier illnesses but he and his wife had lost two of their eight children to scarlet fever. Though dining cars were aboard some eastern trains, this was the wild and woolly west. Fred Harvey, a perfectionist, was determined to make a difference. He created a vision for a system of restaurants along a railroad route, pitched the idea to the Burlington, and was turned down. As the story goes, a Burlington official said, "Ask the Santa Fe. They'll try anything."

Indeed, Santa Fe executives listened; liked what they heard; and on January 1, 1878, struck the first of decades of deals with Fred Harvey. By 1939, 50 lunch and dining rooms were along Santa Fe routes. Mirroring Harvey's personal style, all were well managed and ran with impeccable efficiency. When a steam locomotive chugged into a station for a 30-minute stop, passengers deboarded to the smiles of the Harvey Girls, who served delicious meals with excellent service.

Fred Harvey took great pride in his young servers and dispelled critics' claims that they were "only waitresses." These women, some 5,000 between 1880 and 1950, worked long, hard shifts at least six days a week. Half of the Harvey Girls stayed in the West after they left the extended Harvey family; many married railroad men and helped develop the towns along the tracks.

Harvey's empire, continued by his sons and grandsons, was not limited to the restaurants. It included two dozen hotels, Indian Detours tourism trips, souvenir shops, and newsstands. Importantly, 30 dining cars on Santa Fe passenger trains continued the Fred Harvey tradition of excellence on the rails.

The era of the Harvey Houses had waned by 1939, and for several reasons. Streamlined passenger trains no longer made the number of stops of their steam predecessors. Many had dining cars. World War II changed the dynamic of passenger service, as did increasing travel by highway and air. Though the shuttling of troops via rail during the war gave some Harvey properties a boost, many closed in the 1930s, with more to follow.

But for many years, Harvey's railroad partner benefited: advertisements boasted, "Only the Santa Fe includes meals by Fred Harvey." He had created the United States' first restaurant chain, and a few popular Harvey hotels and dining spots still operate today.

network. Think what the railroad world would be like if chief mechanical officers could select the shape and height above the rails of the coupler for the locomotives and cars under their jurisdictions. Given the chance, some just might decide to be different!

As we ride west here in 1939, the Santa Fe and all other railroads have been bearing for a long time an immense burden of economic regulation by the federal government. So intrusive upon their business has been the Interstate Commerce Commission (ICC) that without its assent a railroad has little to say that's final about what markets it may enter or leave, what it may charge its customers, and the degree to which it is permitted to be competitive. One might hear frustrated railroad executives declare that about all the authority they have is deciding what times their trains may leave. They really aren't that constrained, but in truth they're as much caretakers as entrepreneurs.

More than one occupant of a high railroad office will observe that those running the railroads now could never have built them. More than one will note that railroads seem to prefer to compete among themselves rather than with the long-haul motor-carrier industry that's driving off with so much of their profit. Largely, that circumstance arises from the dulling effect of federal transportation policies that date to well before the beginning of the 20th century. From where we are today in 1939, it'll be a l-o-n-g time before government begins to treat railroads no more possessively—is *no more negatively* too strong a term?—than it treats other private businesses, including competition from other transportation modes.

Railroads long have seen government tilt the playing field to the advantage of trucks and barges. Why? Politics, of course, and a bad reputation the railroads hardly deserve. However powerful are the combined forces of the railroads and their suppliers and supporters, the political power of the nation's motor-carrier industry and its allies can outvote the railroad industry every time.

Facing top, In a 1926 photo, customers and staff pose inside the dining room at the Harvey House in Hutchinson, Kansas. *Photo Santa Fe Railway, kansasmemory.org, Kansas Historical Society*

Besides, the government certainly couldn't bring itself to spend tax dollars to benefit private railroad corporations that are deemed to have been unethical, to say the least, back in the days when they were developing the country and were the only medium of overland transport save for the horse, mule, and ox. It's much easier, and it's far more acceptable politically, to spend public moneys on highways, waterways, and airways. Never mind a lot of what government spends that way is derived from taxes the railroads pay.

The tainted competitive atmosphere has been around so long most career railroaders hardly realize a better way could exist. Over the industry lies the pall of generations of federal and state constraints. So too lies a deeply ingrained unionism, a massive and monstrously expensive fixed plant, and a stifling traditionalism. Seniority and pecking order seem sometimes as important to railroad management as they do to unionized employees.

But then, again, here's this remarkable *Super Chief* we're riding. And here, in conjunction with a major manufacturer of automobiles, we find the Santa Fe about to shake the railroad industry's venerable motive-power establishment to its very foundations. Maybe there's hope.

The Santa Fe is a big railroad. In this year 1939, as in every year, it'll change in size, but just a little. It touches lightly, runs the length or breadth of, or, in some instances, casts a web of tracks over 12 states. In total mileage, a fraction more than 13,443, it ranks first among United States railroads. It regards as its primary routes its main lines from Chicago through Kansas City westward, reaching the Pacific Ocean through California, and extending southward through Texas to the Gulf of Mexico. Its secondary and branch lines live mostly off the agricultural, mineral, and industrial economies through which they pass. While they comprise roughly two-thirds of total system mileage, these lines generate only about a third of total system revenues.

Among its many sources of dollars, the Santa Fe counts Kansas grain elevators, Texas cotton fields and cattle ranches, Illinois cornfields, California fruit orchards and vegetable farms, Oklahoma oil wells, Colorado mineral mines, traveling Hollywood personalities, businessmen on the move, families on

Facing, An archway of Albuquerque's Spanish Mission-style station frames a passenger walking to board the *El Capitan*. *Photo Wallace W. Abbey,* Trains *magazine, Kalmbach Media*

Above, In a publicity photo at Dearborn Station, an engineer, or more likely a professional model, waves from the cab of Santa Fe's 1A and 1B diesels of 1935, on the head end of the *Super Chief*. *Photo Santa Fe Railway, Wallace W. Abbey Collection*

Facing, Double-headed 2900-class 4-8-4s drift into the receiving yard at Argentine, outside Kansas City, with an eastbound freight train. *Photo Wallace W. Abbey,* Trains *magazine, Kalmbach Media*

Above, The operator at Turner, Kansas, hoops up train orders to the head brakeman as the fireman on the 2-8-2 looks on. *Photo Santa Fe Railway, Wallace W. Abbey Collection*

The names and numbers of dozens of crewmen and steam locomotives occupy the call board at Wellington, Kansas, in 1943. *Photo Jack Delano, Prints & Photographs Division, Library of Congress*

their way to see the grandparents, and students on their way to college. The Santa Fe takes business to, and receives business from, myriad connecting railroads both on the perimeter of its territory and at many points in its interior.

The Santa Fe and all other railroads are required to report the composition of their freight traffic to their principal regulator, the ICC. So we know that, among the many commodities it will transport in 1939, the Santa Fe will handle 3,440,475 tons of wheat; 436 tons of live poultry; 3,178,462 tons of refined petroleum products; 102,061 tons of passenger automobiles; 1,731,282 tons of bituminous coal and 17,165 tons of anthracite; 532 tons of butterine (an artificial butter) and margarine; 654,390 tons of cattle and calves in single-deck cars and 18,000 tons in double-deck cars; 8,609 tons of hogs in single-deck cars and 63,915 tons in double-deck cars; and 526,000 tons of oranges and grapefruit.

It may be unfair to say it this way, but the ICC doesn't seem interested in how much money the Santa Fe makes, or loses, handling this business. It publishes statistics principally on how much the business weighs.

Carload traffic in total will weigh 30.5 million tons in 1939. Less-than-carload traffic, no railroad's favorite even now, will add 518,000 tons. Nothing resembling "intermodal" traffic exists, although the Santa Fe Railway does have its own truck lines: Santa Fe Transportation Company in California, and Santa Fe Trail Transportation Company in seven states within truck reach of such cities as Kansas City. In many communities, including some that aren't on its tracks, trucks marked with the Santa Fe cross pick up "LCL" and bring it down to the depot, where it is loaded by hand into boxcars. The idea that a railroad might benefit by collaborating with long-haul truckers has yet to occur.

Before the Depression, the Santa Fe employed as many as 82,000 people, but as we ride across the system here in 1939, there are only about 33,000. Over the period of our story, we'll see far greater numbers draw Santa Fe paychecks as the domestic impact of world conflict lands squarely on this railroad. In 1944, 64,000 employees will be on the war-swollen payroll.

As if we hadn't experienced magic enough on this trip, pick up that modest little booklet there on the side table. It's the Forty-Fifth Annual Report of the Atchison, Topeka and Santa Fe Railway Company for the Year Ended December 31, 1939.

Let's see what this annual report can tell us.

That employee head count is of much less relative significance in 1939 than it will be in years to come seems to be indicated by its scant mention in the annual report. The document comments only on a recent policy requiring officers to retire by age 70. This prompted many changes in the official roster during the year.

The year 1939 went—will go, rather—into the records as a pretty successful one. There's been significant progress financially in the climb out of the Depression. While in no way will annual profit achieve the 1931 level of $23.1 million, 1939's net corporate income of $8.5 million will be the highest since 1935 and 1936.

The Depression years reversed a trend for Santa Fe's net income to soar. In 1929 the company totted up a net income of more than $61 million, but by 1933 the railroad's net stood at a mere $3.7 million. Since then, net income has managed to climb by about a million dollars a year. Throughout the Depression, the Santa Fe told its shareholders its railroad was in good repair. It was even able to spend some money on improvements.

About 80 percent of operating revenues will come from moving freight. Passenger revenues will account for 11 percent. Mail, express, and miscellaneous revenues will produce the balance. The 1939 balance sheet will be clear of debt, save for funded long-term obligations of $332 million and current liabilities of $19.9 million.

The Santa Fe will finish the year 1939 with $74.5 million in current assets, $34.7 million of which will be cash. The 18,000-plus holders of its preferred stock received a dividend totaling more than $3.1 million in August 1939, and they'll get another of like amount in February 1940.

On average, a ton of revenue freight will move 376.8 miles and gross $4.11. On average, passengers will travel 398.1 miles and pay the Santa Fe an average of $7.04 to get them where they're going. The distance in either case is less than that from Chicago

Facing, Navajo members of a track gang align the rails during a welded-rail installation near Gallup, New Mexico. *Photo Santa Fe Railway, kansasmemory.org, Kansas Historical Society*

Above, In a late 1930s image, sleek E1 No. 3 shares track space with B units at the 21st Street engine facility in Chicago. *Photo Santa Fe Railway, Barriger National Railroad Library, St. Louis Mercantile Library at University of Missouri-St. Louis*

In a prewar photograph, an unidentified Los Angeles–bound passenger train behind 4-8-2 No. 3744 poses in Cajon Pass. *Photo Santa Fe Railway, kansasmemory.org, Kansas Historical Society*

The interlocking tower at Holliday, Kansas, as viewed from the rear platform of a westbound passenger train. *Photo John W. Barriger III, Barriger National Railroad Library, St. Louis Mercantile Library at University of Missouri-St. Louis*

to Kansas City. (And this is a "long-haul" railroad?) All told, the Santa Fe in 1939 will perform 42,127,111 train-miles of transportation service. Freight train-miles will exceed passenger train-miles by a mere million. Relative to the freight traffic, that's a lot of passenger train-miles!

At the close of 1939, Santa Fe will have in service 1,600 locomotives, of which 1,546 will be steam driven: 1,119 oil-burners and 427 coal-burners. It will roster 76,212 freight cars, with 25,980 boxcars dominating the fleet and 14,064 refrigerator cars being second. Coal cars, 11,732 of them, come in third. There are 8,464 stock cars, 5,808 automobile-carrying boxcars, 3,398 railroad-owned oil tank cars, and 2,500 flat cars. Ballast, caboose and drover, concentrate, ice, log, and tie cars complete the roster.

Santa Fe's passenger and head-end (baggage, mail, and express) business is supported by 1,355 cars. There are 491 coach cars in various configurations and 36 smoking cars. Seventy-two dining cars, 36 lounge cars, 18 club cars, 15 parlor cars, and 9 café-observation cars put considerable class into the fleet.

Too Many Santa Fes!

Another 535 cars carry baggage, mail, and express parcels. Not that they'd show up on the *Super Chief*, but the Santa Fe also owns 42 express refrigerator cars and 20 horse express cars.

Most of the sleeping cars it runs belong to the Pullman Company, but the Santa Fe does roster five sleepers of its own. One might surmise these are the cars of the new *Super Chief*, Santa Fe owned but Pullman operated.

That the trains sometimes shouldn't stop when the track runs out prompts the Santa Fe to own five steam tugboats and five car floats in San Francisco Bay.

At the end of the year the Santa Fe will own 4,275 pieces of company-service equipment. Given that this is 1939, few indeed are rubber-tired highway or hi-rail vehicles. Most ride the rails on flanged steel wheels.

We're not far past the beginning of the diesel revolution. Santa Fe's first diesel-electric, a switcher, came in 1935. In this year 1939, 30 diesel-electrics have been acquired for switching and passenger service. The dieselized *Tulsan* went into operation on December 10; the *Kansas Cityan* and *Chicagoan* were extended from Wichita to Oklahoma City the same day. To meet need and public preference, in 1939 the Santa Fe added dining cars to some trains that had been stopping for meals at Harvey Houses.

The diesel-electrics on the Santa Fe's roster will run a total of 2,162,564 train-miles, 16,138,153 car-miles, in 1939. The diesels will consume 17,731 tons of fuel, which cost 6.51 cents per mile, on the average. Whereas a coal-burning steam locomotive can make a little more than 10 miles per ton of fuel and an oil-burner can go almost 22, diesels will average better than 181 miles per ton—on a different kind of fuel, to be sure.

During 1939, 1,575 new freight cars and 226 new pieces of company-service equipment will go to work. A total of 98 steam locomotives, 10 locomotive tenders, 3,530 freight cars, 17 passenger cars, and 319 pieces of company-service equipment will be retired.

When hostilities broke out in Europe in September 1939, American railroads agreed to prepare for heavier traffic, to avoid the pitfalls of equipment shortages that befell the industry as World War I erupted in 1914. This year, the Santa Fe has ordered some $10 million in freight cars for delivery in 1940: 1,800 boxcars, 450 refrigerator cars, 200 ballast cars, 250 gondolas, and 100 flat cars.

The Santa Fe will be a little shorter at the end of 1939 than it was at the end of 1938: 8.37 miles, net. Gone will be 30 miles of branch lines in Oklahoma, New Mexico, and Arizona. Added will be two lines in California, the Magunden and Oil City branches, as the Santa Fe takes its every-other-year turn at operating them. It owns them jointly with the Southern Pacific.

Up to 1939, rail that weighed 131 pounds to the yard had been confined to places where the demands on the track were particularly severe. During 1939 that weight was made standard on the main line between Chicago and Los Angeles. Sixteen miles of it and 327 miles of 112-pound rail replaced older rail. Plans were made to lay 105 miles of 131-pound and 218 miles of 112-pound rail during 1940.

For as dry as much of its territory usually is, the Santa Fe spent nearly $1.5 million in 1939 to repair damage caused by successive heavy autumn rains in western Arizona and southeastern California. It still needs to spend an equal amount. In some locations it's moving the railroad to avoid future floods. It's planning a branch line to a new potash crusher and refinery in the Pecos River valley near Carlsbad, New Mexico, the third such installation since 1931. Domestic sources of this important mineral are replacing European sources cut off by international conflict.

In the June 1940 to come, construction already underway in Arizona between Joseph City and Double Track Junction out near Winslow will close the last single-track gap in the otherwise twin-track main line of the Coast Lines. The Santa Fe then will say it has either double track or two separate single-track routes from Chicago all the way to California. No other railroad in the transcontinental trade can make that claim.

The annual report doesn't say it this way, but figuratively, and perhaps operationally, in 1939 the Santa Fe is held together more by copper line wire than by most anything else. Trains get up and down the railroad mostly on the authority of telegraphed or telephoned train orders, clearance cards, and other such written instructions that move from pole to pole over wires along the tracks. The common method of communication, particularly in the hinterlands, is by Morse code, private party-line telephone, or Teletype systems.

Hand or lantern signals often are the only means of communicating, one employee to another. Train-to-train, train-to-wayside station, or employee-to-employee radio won't enter the picture for years. If people are thinking up the internet, they are probably afraid to mention it. Besides, they're waiting for someone to invent the computer.

Define geographically and climatologically a territory through which a railroad might operate and doubtless you'll define an environment that surrounds some of the Santa Fe. The Santa Fe is a prairie railroad, a mountain railroad, a Granger line, an industrial railroad, a trunk line that runs through hundreds of miles of sparsely settled countryside. In elevation it climbs from near the shore of Lake Michigan and from near the levels of the Pacific Ocean and the Gulf of Mexico to considerable heights in Colorado, New Mexico, and Arizona. Among many scenic delights the Santa Fe crosses the Flint Hills of Kansas, the Piney Woods of Texas, and the gentle beauty of the Tehachapi Mountains in California.

If anything distinguishes the Santa Fe from the other railroads in the western trade, it would be its grades, particularly in New Mexico, Arizona, and California. Out west on the Northern District is where our Model Fs will first go to school. Classes will be tough.

Railroad civil engineers tend to concern themselves at least as much with total rise and fall over a given lineal distance as they do with how vertical the track might be on the slope of a given mountain. With its successive long and steep grades, the Arizona Divide country is the Santa Fe's most difficult piece of railroad to operate.

At the turn of the century, Santa Fe established 1.42 percent, just under a foot and a half per 100 feet, as its preferred maximum ruling grade. In flatter regions, the standard was set at 0.6 percent. Here in 1939 the Santa Fe meets its own mountain standard most everywhere except over Raton and Glorieta Passes in New Mexico and eastward from Ash Fork up to Supai in Arizona. To help meet the standards, the Southern District was opened for through traffic in 1908. In many places there a second main track has been constructed on more forgiving uphill grades.

Severity of grade is thus defined by the Santa Fe: Grades of up to 0.3 percent are regarded as water level. Light grades are those that rise or fall at the rate of 0.3 to 0.5 percent, moderate grades at 0.6 to 0.9 percent, heavy grades from 1.0 to 1.5 percent. By definition, mountain grades are those greater than 1.5 percent.

And then there are the curves. To pick an extreme example, there are more than 120 curves in the 150 miles between Williams and Seligman in Arizona. On the descent from the Arizona Divide summit westward, they're sharp and almost continuous. A 10-degree curve is sharp enough—a radius of only 573.7 feet—to restrict train speed severely. As we ride westward, nearly all the curves between Williams and Seligman are sharper than 2 degrees. Between these two stations, 21 curves measure 10 degrees or sharper. The Santa Fe's preferred standard is 2 degrees, a 2,865-foot radius. In 1941, it will become 1 degree, a 5,730-foot radius. Changes aside, all these successive curves remain a challenge for locomotive engineers charged with delivering a smooth ride.

The service of our *Super Chief* and its staff is efficient and flawless. It suggests the Santa Fe is one big, well-organized operation. But the Santa Fe really consists of an aggregation of shorter, somewhat independent, generally but not always cooperating railroads connected largely end to end. While this pattern dare not annoy the extra-fare passengers, the "family tree" of traditional railroad organization and management makes any continuous operation the length of the system—such as moving a *Super Chief* or a *Northern California Fast Freight* between its termini—more awkward, less efficient, and more expensive than it might be.

A railroad's operations are influenced, too, by the capabilities of its locomotives. The Santa Fe of 1939 is designed around steam power, of course. For all its merits, and even though since 1920 it's been doing much to overthrow the labor-prompted requirement that the locomotive be changed every time the crew changes, the steam locomotive generally is not a long-distance runner. The Santa Fe is ripe for a form of motive power that is.

Corporately speaking, there are three "Santa Fes": the Atchison, Topeka and Santa Fe, known in some official circles as the AT&SF proper, which includes the Coast Lines; the Gulf, Colorado & Santa Fe (GC&SF); and the Panhandle & Santa Fe (P&SF). The GC&SF and the Panhandle are wholly owned subsidiaries of the AT&SF that operate trains in Texas according to state laws.

The just over 13,000 miles of the Santa Fe system are broken down as follows: The AT&SF operates 9,468 main-line miles and owns 9,197. The GC&SF operates 2,103 and owns 2,106. The P&SF operates 1,825 and owns 1,869. Each company has its own management; territory; physical structure; and, sometimes, corporate culture.

Operationally speaking, the Santa Fe is divided, not altogether along corporate lines, into four grand divisions, regional in nature: Eastern Lines; Western Lines (including the Panhandle & Santa Fe); Gulf, Colorado & Santa Fe; and Coast Lines.

The Eastern Lines subdivide into Eastern and Western Districts. The Western Lines are split into the Northern and Southern Districts, over which our magical *Super Chief* now rides.

The grand divisions include 20 operating divisions, often further divided into main-line districts about the length of a freight engineer's tour of duty, on the order of 100 miles.

Now we've gotten down to where we should recognize how the Santa Fe functions. Each operating division, and to some extent, each district, supplements the grand division general office with a large and rather complete administrative staff: superintendent; master mechanic; civil, mechanical, and other engineers; claims agents; storekeepers; accountants and auditors; trainmasters; road foremen of engines; clerks; and many others in diverse occupations. From most every division point, dispatchers control the movement of trains.

Somewhere on each division is at least one major locomotive terminal. Each of the grand divisions has at least one backshop capable of performing heavy work on locomotives. The idea of farming out the repair or reconstruction of locomotives or cars is unheard of, and it would be impractical if it were attempted. Who out there besides a locomotive builder or car builder, or another railroad, could do the work? And what would the Santa Fe's own shop-craft unions say about that?

Facilities of some size and capacity for working on freight and passenger cars are either located with the locomotive shops or at sites somewhere else on each grand division. Nearby are huge storehouses and machine shops filled with whatever's needed to run a railroad.

While the corporate complexity is largely the outgrowth of expansion and tradition, Texas is responsible for some of it. By state law, a railroad operating in Texas must have its general office in Texas. Thus, in addition to four general offices—the AT&SF's in Chicago, the Eastern Lines' in Topeka, the Western Lines' and P&SF's in Amarillo, and the Coast Lines' in Los Angeles—there's a fifth office for the GC&SF in Galveston. It won't be until 1964 that the requirement for a Texas general office will disappear, paving the way for considerable simplification in the uppermost levels of the organization chart.

And where, specifically, is this Southern District? Call it the Belen Cutoff and you'll better understand. The Cutoff leaves the Northern District main line at Ellinor, 13 miles west of Emporia, Kansas. As part of the Middle, Panhandle, Plains, and Pecos Divisions, it reaches the Coast Lines at Belen. Three of the Cutoff's seven districts belong to the Southern District of the Western Lines, hence the nickname.

—⁂—

Mostly, here in 1939, the Santa Fe's locomotives—almost all steam, remember—are assigned individually to a given division, or more specifically to a given shop, for maintenance. Rarely will they wander so far from their home shop that they couldn't be sent back for periodic inspection. The practice will continue into the days of the FTs, although in due course there'll be far fewer major shops. The diesel shops often will be at locations other than those of the big steam shops.

Except on some through trains, mostly passenger, locomotive engineers and firemen usually work no more than the length of their home territory. By agreements with the unions, an incoming freight crew must deliver its locomotive to the outgoing crew at the roundhouse, even when no work on the train requires that the locomotive be uncoupled. Train crews generally work territories defined at the beginning of the 20th century by how far the locomotives of the time could run in a working day, although on some through passenger runs the train crew might cover longer

At the grade at Quinlan, Oklahoma, 4-8-4 No. 2901 is down to 15 mph as it pushes west with Second 23, the *Grand Canyon Limited*. Photo Preston George, Everette Lee DeGolyer Jr. Collection of US Railroad Photographs, DeGolyer Library, Southern Methodist University

distances than do the engine crews. Track-maintenance crews, or section gangs, are assigned to relatively short stretches of line.

Introducing diesels to freight service will begin to change many of the ways the Santa Fe of 1939 operates.

―⁂―

Well, look at that! We're there! Our *Super Chief* is pulling into Los Angeles Union Station, newly opened for trains of the Santa Fe, Southern Pacific, and Union Pacific. One of these future days, the first of the Santa Fe's new freight diesels will be in and out of here with trains of dignitaries and the press before it goes into its appointed service. But for now, thank you, magical *Super Chief*. We won't be going back with you. Before those new diesels arrive, we've more exploring to do on this aggregation of too many railroads called the Santa Fe.

Too Many Santa Fes!

A pair of 2-8-2s lugs a westbound freight up Olathe Hill, Kansas, a favorite haunt of the author in his college years. *Photo Wallace W. Abbey, Center for Railroad Photography & Art Collection*

THREE MECHANICAL MOTION, SET TO MUSIC

Santa Fe Steam at the Dawn of the FT

SOME THINGS YOU'LL REMEMBER ALWAYS. ME, I'LL ALWAYS remember the sounds of the Santa Fe's steam locomotives. Of course, I *try* to remember them. Wouldn't you?

I remember…

…as a kid, lying awake on a humid summer night in my grandparents' house in Cherryvale in southeast Kansas, the chant of the engine on what we called the "CC&B," the "Cherryvale, Coffeyville & Back," as it switches in the yard three blocks down the street; the sound swelling up as the train crew prepares to kick a car, subsiding to the *ta-bonk-a-bonk-shee* of the air compressor and the whine of steam escaping the turbo-generator…

…as a teenager, well out toward the end of a platform at Dearborn Station, the tentative first exhalation of a shiny black Pacific as, his eyes fixed on the track beneath his window, the engineer urges his steed to move the *Grand Canyon Limited* first an inch and then away from Chicago…

…as a student riding to Kansas during World War II in the crowded lounge car of the *Grand Canyon*, there being no room in the chair cars, without air-conditioning and with the window open and funneling dust and grime; the on-beat, off-beat syncopation of two big Pacifics, their stack extensions scraping the Missouri sky…

…as a soon-to-be-graduated Jayhawker doing quiet-hours telephone duty next to an open window in a dorm on Mount Oread; the approach across the Wakarusa Valley of the first section of the westbound *Grand Canyon*, its whistle screaming, warning all of Lawrence its coming, as it meets the first section of the eastbound *California Limited*; the conversation-by-steam-whistle between the two engineers as they greet each other down by the dark river:

"Ta-wowww… Wow! Wow!"

"Whoop! Whoop! Ta-wowww… Wow! Wow!"

"Whoop! Whoop!"

I knew what the engineers were saying to each other. His train being superior by timetable direction, the engineer of the first section of eastbound 4 had whistled first. With a long and two shorts, he'd called westbound First 23's attention to the green signals that First 4 was displaying, signifying that another section was following. The engineer of First 23 had acknowledged with two shorts. He'd then signaled that he, too, was being followed by another section. The engineer of First 4 had acknowledged his advice.

It was important information, and it was music. That's one thing a steam locomotive did well: it could set mechanical motion to music.

―――

What would someone recall about the Santa Fe's larger steam locomotives in the days when the diesels that would replace them were just coming on?

How big they were, certainly, and in locomotive terms, how big boned: Giant boilers. Fireboxes in which you could've set up housekeeping were the climate not hotter than Kansas in summer. You could measure one of those beautiful beasts by its technical specifications—weight on drivers, tractive effort,

Engine 3427, one of 50 4-6-2s built by Baldwin between 1919 and 1924, leads the eastbound *Hopi* out of Kansas City Union Station on September 13, 1931. *Photo Otto C. Perry, Western History Collection, The Denver Public Library*

evaporative surface—and still not comprehend its size nor understand from where it derived its power.

Tall driving wheels, 7 feet in diameter on the fastest passenger locomotives; 80 inches on 4-8-4s that didn't care whether they were pulling freight or passengers, it made no difference to them; 74 inches—6 foot, 2 inches, taller than most men!—on 2-10-4s that dwarfed everything around them.

But for all their size, Santa Fe steam locomotives, at least the later and larger ones, had nice lines.

Their tenders were the size of barns. There was more than enough room on their sides for the company name in giant letters above a road number you could read all the way across the yard. Inside could be as many as 24,500 gallons of the West's precious water and more than 7,000 gallons of oil for fuel.

The family resemblance was strong, class to class. The smokebox would be lagged and jacketed, just like the boiler. You could bet on a flat smokebox front with a visorless Golden Glow headlight in the center, the road number beneath it. The

One of Santa Fe's regal 2900-class 4-8-4s departs Belen, New Mexico, on January 12, 1947, with the eastbound *Scout*. Photo Otto C. Perry, Western History Collection, The Denver Public Library

sand dome—sometimes there'd be more than one—was huge. Cross-compound air pumps and other appliances might be arrayed on the pilot beam, protected sometimes by shields that, from head-on, made the locomotive look as if it were kneeling. There'd be boxes somewhere up around the stack, backlit at night, displaying the engine's road number. There'd be a deep-throated whistle, a churchlike bell.

Regardless of how modern the engine was, though, its pilot, riveted up out of what looked to be boiler tubing, would seem antique. The pattern did go back to the days of wood-slat pilots. But what an economical way to build a part that could be subjected to more than a little distress.

Variations existed within the family appearance, to be sure, depending on the engine's age, size, and service. But, so said the Santa Fe's steam locomotives, we're big engines designed to handle big trains across a big country.

Of course, it hadn't always been like that.

Mechanical Motion, Set to Music

Like most railroads, the Santa Fe had started out in the late 1800s largely with 4-4-0 American Standards and 2-6-0 Moguls. In these early days of steam, the Santa Fe acquired its motive power largely from Taunton Locomotive Works or Hinkley and Pittsburgh Works, companies with their own ideas about what to build onto a locomotive and where to hang it. Many separate classes existed. Standardization wasn't a strong influence.

Over time, motive power got bigger and heavier and began to develop a few family traits, not all of which were conventional.

Consider, for example, a decidedly unconventional fleet on the Santa Fe roster: 956 locomotives that extracted energy in the steam they generated not once but twice. This practice of "compounding" was commonplace in stationary and marine steam engines of the time, but it had never really taken hold in locomotives except here and there on big freight hogs. On the Santa Fe, though, compounding put in a sizable appearance.

The first compound was built by Schenectady Locomotive Works in 1890, with more to follow from other builders, especially from the Baldwin Locomotive Works and Santa Fe's own Topeka Shop. Ultimately, compounds came in just about every wheel arrangement known to the Santa Fe, and in most common varieties—balanced, cross, Mallet, tandem, and Vauclain. They ranged from lethargic freight helpers to leggy passenger speedsters. The last were balanced-compound 4-6-2s of the 3500 class.

John Player, Santa Fe's machinery superintendent during the era of the compounds, did much to champion their development.

Facing, In a 1915-era photo, a 2-6-2 Prairie-type and a Ten-Wheeler lead a freight train out of Staffordville, Kansas. *Everette Lee DeGolyer Jr. Collection of US Railroad Photographs, DeGolyer Library, Southern Methodist University*

Above, Named for the railroad: a 2-10-2 Santa Fe, likely in helper service, lumbers through Cajon Pass as the crew glances at the photographer. *Everette Lee DeGolyer Jr. Collection of US Railroad Photographs, DeGolyer Library, Southern Methodist University*

Ten-coupled locomotives arrived in 1901 in the form of tandem-compound 2-10-0s to serve primarily as helpers on the heavier grades. They worked fine, but with no trailing truck to guide the driving wheels in reverse, they tended to derail when backing up. And so, in 1903 the 2-10-2 Santa Fe wheel arrangement was born, so named because no other railroad used this configuration for a number of years. The Santa Fe's claim was that these locomotives were the world's largest.

Several classes of articulated compound—think of two locomotives sharing one boiler—were constructed new. They seemed to have swallowed existing locomotives, which is more or less what had happened. For a while, the Santa Fe thought this was a great way to increase the service life of obsolescent machines.

Arguably, the most unusual steam locomotives to go into Santa Fe service were 10 compound articulated engines with

Mechanical Motion, Set to Music

2-10-10-2 wheel arrangements. When they arrived in 1911, they, too, were billed by the Santa Fe as the largest in the world. Each consisted of the boiler, firebox, and cab of an existing 2-10-2 and a new front half that looked like more of the boiler but contained other devices essential to the production of huge volumes of steam.

In 1912, John Purcell had become Santa Fe's head of motive power. Purcell had joined Santa Fe's Mechanical Department at age 14. Among his innovations was a larger tender for the steam locomotive to reduce water stops along the route. Over the years, Purcell brought to the Santa Fe the concepts of standardization and interchangeability of parts across several types and classes of locomotives.

Purcell also oversaw important operational developments. Unlike many roads that looked to the builders to work out the details of new locomotives, in 1915 the Santa Fe began placing its own mechanical-engineering talent at Baldwin, literally sitting next to the experts. Their job was to satisfy the superiors that the plans and specifications drawn in Topeka were guiding the manufacturer in Philadelphia.

In 1915, too, came the 3600, a 4-6-2 that looked like a fat 3500-class compound and that now and then pulled a passenger train. The Santa Fe had commissioned it to be a static exhibit at the Panama-Pacific International Exposition in San Francisco. The first single-expansion locomotive to join the roster in many years, the 3600 did not live up to its billing.

Facing, An impossibly long—and ultimately unsuccessful—2-10-10-2, the world's largest locomotive when built in 1911, poses at San Bernardino, California. *Everette Lee DeGolyer Jr. Collection of US Railroad Photographs, DeGolyer Library, Southern Methodist University*

Above, A pair of 4-8-2s is working hard as they struggle through Raton Pass with a westbound freight at Wootton, Colorado. *Photo Santa Fe Railway, kansasmemory.org, Kansas Historical Society*

Facing, Amid a cloud of brakeshoe smoke, 4-6-2 No. 3425 and train 23, the *Grand Canyon,* descend the grade east of Wilburn, Illinois, on October 22, 1941. *Photo Frank Naven, Wallace W. Abbey Collection*

Above, Hauling a section of a regular train, 4-8-4 No. 3781 passes the east end of the east siding at Olathe, Kansas. *Photo Wallace W. Abbey, Center for Railroad Photography & Art Collection*

Legend suggested the 3600 did its best work at the Exposition. If it actually got there, that is. An enduring story contended it was delivered to the Santa Fe too late to be put on display. Another story held that when it was in service, the 3600 had the unsettling tendency to want to come into town upside down.

Compounds were much more than an experiment and by no means failures. The 3600, for example, played an important role in the history of Santa Fe steam: that of a prototype. Its advanced-for-the-time design contributed to the excellence of the classes of locomotives that would begin to arrive next.

Mechanical Motion, Set to Music

A 2-10-4 in helper service assists a four-unit set of F7 diesels out of Belen, New Mexico, toward Abo Canyon on June 30, 1957. *Everette Lee DeGolyer Jr. Collection of US Railroad Photographs, DeGolyer Library, Southern Methodist University*

INVENTING THE DIESEL

Theodor and Elise Diesel welcomed their third child into the world on March 18, 1858, doubtless having no idea this new son would turn their name into a household word. Rudolf Diesel's parents were Bavarian, immigrants living in Paris. The Diesel family was of humble means; Theodor made leather goods. Rudolf, who helped in his father's shop after school, was an excellent student who soon showed an aptitude for technology.

Rudolf decided at age 14 he would be an engineer; he graduated at age 16 at the top of his class and enrolled in the Industrial School of Augsburg. There, he was mentored by Professor Carl von Linde, who was exploring techniques of refrigeration. At age 18, Rudolf accepted a merit scholarship at the Royal Bavarian Polytechnic of Munich. When typhoid fever delayed his graduation date—he would graduate with honors—he passed the time working at the Sulzer Brothers Machine Works in Winterthur, Switzerland, a plant that was manufacturing Professor von Linde's refrigeration machines.

Carl von Linde employed Rudolf Diesel for several years and enabled him to gain a number of patents in both Germany and France. Diesel expanded his knowledge beyond refrigeration, researched thermal and fuel efficiency, and built a steam engine using ammonia vapor. During testing, it exploded. A later test of a high-compression iron-and-steel cylinder also exploded. Diesel's young years were marked by frequent hospitalizations.

Diesel spent many years designing an efficient internal-combustion engine. In 1893, he published a paper, "Theory and Construction of a Rational Heat-engine to Replace the Steam Engine and the Combustion Engines Known Today." He applied for a patent but soon realized his initial theory was flawed; he corrected his design and applied for a second patent.

Since more than 90 percent of available energy in a steam engine is wasted, Diesel worked toward much higher efficiency ratios. In his engine, fuel was injected at the end of the compression stroke and was ignited by the high temperature resulting from the compression.

The first successful diesel engine ran in 1897. Sixteen years later, Rudolf Diesel mysteriously disappeared aboard a steamer en route to a conference in London, England. His body was discovered 10 days later. Encyclopedic references and biographies state Diesel's resting place as the North Sea.

After his death, Diesel's namesake engine continued to be developed and refined. Over time, it replaced the steam piston engine in many types of machinery, including agricultural and military equipment; factories; pipelines and water plants; submarines and ships; automobiles; trucks; and, of course, locomotives.

Rudolf Diesel. *Photo Sueddeutsche Zeitung, Alamy Stock Photo*

Still, relatively high maintenance costs, the application of superheaters to other locomotives beginning in 1911, and a test on the Pecos Division in 1920 combined to bring an end to the preoccupation with compounds. The 1920 test showed how a not-so-old single-expansion 3800-class 2-10-2 could produce 35 percent more pulling power than could a compound 2-6-6-2 Prairie Mallet.

Most of the compounds were gone, scrapped, or "simpled"—rebuilt with a single-expansion cylinder—long before World War II. Yet even after the war one could find in service many locomotives that had once been compounds, for there was a time when the Santa Fe owned little else.

Five hundred one new locomotives in six classes, all simple machines, were on the property by 1927. For all practical purposes, the entire herd was Santa Fe designed, built on the Baldwin erecting floor. These locomotives—the 3129, 3160, and 4000 classes of 2-8-2s; the 3400 class of 4-6-2s; the 3700 class of 4-8-2s; the 3800 class of 2-10-2s—exemplified the advancements in Santa Fe steam. By far the best developed of the 2-10-2s were the 141 single-expansion 3800s delivered between 1919 and 1927. They became the standard heavy freight power on the Coast Lines and in other demanding territories. Were they racehorses? Hardly. Draft horses? Yep.

In 1927, too, at Baldwin just short of the last minute, the Santa Fe had the single-axle trailing truck beneath 2-10-2 No. 3829, then under construction, replaced with a two-axle truck. The four-wheel trailing truck had just become available. Its application was not so much an experiment with the resulting 2-10-4 wheel arrangement as it was a test of the truck itself. The result was much better support for the voluminous firebox of No. 3829, the nation's first 2-10-4. The Santa Fe would make no more modifications to the 3800s, not that some weren't contemplated.

Never again would Santa Fe buy a steam locomotive of its own design that didn't have two axles and four wheels under the firebox and cab. Witness the new arrivals during 1927–1930: 10 3450-class 4-6-4s; 15 4101-class 2-8-4s; 14 3751-class 4-8-4s; and a 5000 class, Santa Fe's first locomotive designed from the outset to be a 2-10-4.

One might wonder why Santa Fe didn't pursue single-expansion articulateds, as had Union Pacific with its 4-6-6-4 *Challengers* and 4-8-8-4 *Big Boys*. Was there lingering sensitivity on the Santa Fe about its earlier experience with compound articulateds? Actually, the reason lay in the Santa Fe's operating territory—in the lack of service facilities on the Coast Lines for such monsters, in hundreds of miles where treated or distilled boiler water cost nearly as much as did fuel oil, and in state laws and agreements with labor unions.

Single-expansion articulateds were studied closely; a 1944 locomotive study, not wanting to overlook any possible economy of operations, had proposed two Mallet-type experimentals in 1947 and two more in 1949. Baldwin even plotted out for the Santa Fe a 4-8-8-4 that would have been larger than UP's American Locomotive–built *Big Boy*.

But the state of Arizona limited freight trains to 70 cars, and the unions held some freight trains in California to 2,900 tons. However logical a Santa Fe version of a *Big Boy* might have appeared to be, not until those artificial inhibitions were eliminated could a locomotive of that power and initial cost earn its keep. And by then, steam on the Santa Fe also would be going.

For other operating reasons, too, the full power of steam locomotives even only as big as the 5001s couldn't be used effectively west of Gallup. The 2-10-4s couldn't be double-headed over the spindly bridge that carried the railroad across Canyon Diablo. They were slippery on the grades of the Arizona Divide. They did nothing to alleviate the bad-water or no-water condition of the mountains and deserts through which they passed. In fact, with their huge need to turn water into steam, they probably would have made the supply problem worse.

Eventually, the 2-10-4s were embargoed altogether west of Winslow. A few members of the class had made brief appearances in California upon their delivery, but for all practical purposes, the 5001s were never Coast Lines engines.

Some within the Santa Fe thought its 2-10-4s were every bit as powerful, useful, and economical as were UP's *Big Boys*. One delightful story (which sounds doubtful) was that the starting tractive effort published for the 5001s was actually the tractive effort at about 19 miles an hour, rigged so yardmasters wouldn't be tempted to tie on behind the tender every car headed in the

A variety of Santa Fe steam power covers the floor of the erecting hall at the San Bernardino shops. *Photo Santa Fe Railway,* Trains *magazine, Kalmbach Media*

same direction. The 2-10-4s were designed not for drag service but for manifest trains, the cream of the freight train crop.

Rebuilding older steam locomotives to cut maintenance expenses, boost tractive effort, and sometimes raise maximum speed was a continuing practice for years. Yet even so, and even with its new locomotives, the Santa Fe in 1940 was running mostly on World War I–vintage power, anything but sufficient. As the challenges of arming the Allies and defending democracy began to present themselves, and as traffic levels climbed in response, for what it wanted to be and had to do the Santa Fe was decidedly short of modern locomotives.

These circumstances suggest why the Santa Fe moved decisively to the diesel-electric as its first-line freight-hauler, once

Electro-Motive's Model F proved itself in 1940. Unless it wanted to spend heavily for new steam locomotives and to perpetuate steam for the long period necessary to amortize gracefully its investment in what seemed destined to be a dying technology, the Santa Fe had no choice. New locomotives simply had to come in quantity. It was better that they be diesels.

That the Santa Fe placed orders for 2-10-4s and 4-8-4s during the war was largely because it couldn't get the diesels it wanted as rapidly as it needed them.

Big changes were coming. The FTs expedited the process of retiring and sending to the scrap merchants the steam locomotives that had outlived their economic usefulness. So, too, was ending Santa Fe's collaboration with Baldwin.

Had time not run out on steam, had General Motors not shown up with a bottom-line better locomotive, continuing one more round of improvements might have made Santa Fe's steam the tightest and most efficient in the industry. The railroad had been headed that way for years. Yet, the entire steam fleet was scrap by the 1950s, save for a few representative examples enshrined in parks, museums, and ceremonial service.

It's been said that on the Santa Fe, steam locomotion was a religion. Even as steam was dying, many still saw it as the only real game in town.

Proposals in 1939 and 1947, beyond the 1944 locomotive study, demonstrated that the Mechanical Department was still wreathed in steam. Consider the proposal to modernize 50 3800-class 2-10-2s with 74-inch drivers. Or the mountains of new driving-wheel tires and side rods behind the shop buildings at Topeka well after the diesels had begun to take over. Consider the 10 or so never-applied cast frames to retrofit more 3400 4-6-2s. Or projections for many more 5001-class 2-10-4s. For years, too, Albuquerque Shops kept applying welded boiler shells to locomotives that would never run a revenue mile.

Think also of the $480,000 steam turbine-electric locomotive the board of directors authorized in 1947; the Mechanical Department wanted to see it built so the Santa Fe wouldn't miss any emerging technologies.

But the quiet word was, President Fred Gurley wasn't going to divert the Santa Fe from the course toward dieselization that by 1947 was well laid in. Gurley was merely giving his Mechanical Department a little slack.

Never let it be said, though, that a diesel-electric was in every way better than a steam locomotive of comparable horsepower. It wasn't. Gurley testified in a labor case that sometimes an appreciable margin of savings, diesel over steam, just wasn't there. A diesel's first cost was far greater—twice, perhaps two and a half times the cost of a comparable steam locomotive. A diesel could start a heavy train better and faster, but it couldn't move the train over the road quite as well as could the steam locomotive. Nor could a diesel run for lengthy periods at less than its rather low continuous rating. A diesel, however, was more amenable to far longer periods of service at greatly reduced operating costs, and that was a big factor.

But even if it couldn't do better everything that needed to be done, the steam locomotive had roped and hog-tied hearts and minds much more tightly than had the diesel, even the minds of seasoned railroaders who were paid to look at cost and performance.

There is evidence of this.

Years after he'd retired, no less an advocate of diesels than Gurley asserted that the Santa Fe's 2900-class 4-8-4s should have been retained for passenger service, with diesels used only on the major mountain grades on the transcontinental main line.

Then there's this: As he started 12 5011-class 2-10-4s on their funereal trudge from Chillicothe to the scrap merchant in the late 1950s after they'd come off lease to the Pennsylvania Railroad, a trainmaster who later became president of the Santa Fe . . . cried.

Many on the Santa Fe had heard and had well appreciated the music.

Facing, Double-headed steam locomotives race past a Santa Fe cantilever signal at Hoover, Texas, in 1943. *Everette Lee DeGolyer Jr. Collection of US Railroad Photographs, DeGolyer Library, Southern Methodist University*

FOUR HAMILTON, WINTON, KETTERING

The Evolution of Electro-Motive

THE HISTORY OF THE ELECTRO-MOTIVE DIVISION OF General Motors is fairly straightforward. The history of the diesel-electric locomotive is not. Nor is the history of the diesel engine, the prime mover, as it was first applied to railroad service. It's time to touch on the high spots along the path from the earliest diesel engines to the relative monsters that came out of Electro-Motive: the Model Fs.

At the time of the Santa Fe's FTs, Electro-Motive was a young son of multiple fathers, all honorable and well intentioned, who got along with each other fine, mostly.

One we'd call a start-up today. It was formed by two men who tried to revive an idea long demonstrated to be unworkable: rail-guided self-propelled conveyances that combined power unit, baggage space, sometimes mail and express space, and sometimes passenger seating, all in the same car body, all on the same wheels. General Electric had tried this but had abandoned the idea in 1918, writing off $1.5 million in losses.

Calling itself the Electro-Motive Engineering Company when it opened its doors—its *door*, perhaps; it was very small, planning to job out the actual construction of its cars—the start-up was incorporated in Cleveland on August 31, 1922. *Engineering* came out of its name in 1923; the term attracted too many inquiries that had nothing to do with railroads, which were where its founders wanted to go.

Electro-Motive was the creation of Harold L. (Hal) Hamilton, a regional sales and service manager for White Motor Company who'd once been a callboy on the Southern Pacific. Hamilton was a self-taught machinist experienced in early gas-electric cars, an attempt to adapt highway trucks to railroad service. Using the small gasoline and diesel engines of the time, he tried to transmit power to the driving axles by mechanical means. He was unsuccessful.

Hamilton and Paul Turner, a White Motor salesman, started Electro-Motive on their faith that a gas-electric prime mover and an electric transmission backed by manufacturer-provided service would give railroads a self-propelled car they could appreciate. The Electro-Motive-powered railcars would be manufactured by J. G. Brill; Bethlehem Steel; Osgood-Bradley; Pullman Standard; Standard Steel Car; and, in the majority, St. Louis Car Company.

Another progenitor of Electro-Motive was Winton Engine Company, a large, well-established manufacturer of engines that ran on gasoline, diesel, and a heavier petroleum product called diesel distillate. With the approximate consistency of kerosene, distillate cost about a third of what gasoline cost.

Winton's engines, used mainly in marine and stationary applications, could reduce by at least two-thirds the immense weight per horsepower of early diesel engines by welding both the engine block and the crankcase rather than by casting them. Winton, also based in Cleveland, would build hundreds of prime

---

Facing, Charles Kettering. *Courtesy Kettering University Archives*

movers, not necessarily of the diesel persuasion, including those for early Electro-Motive products such as Union Pacific's *M-10000*, the Burlington's *Zephyr*, the Santa Fe's "Amos 'n Andy," and other switching and passenger locomotives.

The third father of Electro-Motive was a huge, multifaceted organization that turned out automobiles by the thousands on long assembly lines and produced a variety of other products: General Motors Corporation, of course. In Detroit, inside General Motors, was an individual who certainly qualified for the role of godfather to the diesel-electric locomotive, if not a role as cofounding father. Charles F. Kettering was an inventor, genius, practical joker, and raconteur. Hired straight out of college by National Cash Register (NCR), Kettering would amass 23 patents in five years, including for the electric cash register in 1906.

Kettering's interests in improving the automobile led him to gather fellow NCR engineers together on nights and weekends, in another guy's barn. The group became known as the Barn Gang and earned Kettering the nickname Boss Ket. By 1909, Kettering had left NCR and founded Dayton Engineering Laboratories Company, Delco. There, among his inventions was the automobile self-starter. When Delco was sold to General Motors in 1918, Kettering became vice president of its Research Corporation, a position he held for 27 years. He would receive 163 more patents, including for the first incubator for premature infants. Kettering would be key to the development of a diesel-electric locomotive prime mover.

We must also include as a precursor to Electro-Motive its future competitor, General Electric (GE), where Hamilton had worked and had learned. GE engines had powered early railcars, including those of the McKeen Company. Before World War I, GE was building diesel engines. Its electrical components would go into early Electro-Motive switching and passenger locomotives. When Electro-Motive began building its own electrical transmissions, it used essentially what were improved versions of GE designs.

Hamilton, Kettering, and others, inventors and visionaries, would collaborate to design a new engine that would change the railroad industry. The steam locomotive's external-combustion engine burned its fuel in a loosely confined space and applied the energy created in an indirect way. Now, Rudolf Diesel had invented the internal-combustion engine that burned its fuel—gasoline, light petroleum oil, powdered coal, in tests even corn oil—in a closed chamber. The pressure of the rapidly expanding products of combustion would push pistons to turn a crankshaft, which then turned the rotor of an electric generator. The gains in fuel efficiency would be enormous.

The internal-combustion engine was capturing the fancy of many people and organizations outside of Cleveland and Detroit. The first internal-combustion locomotive built in North America might have been the 1898 product of the Patton Motor Company in Chicago, a heat-ignition engine mounted in a small railway car manufactured by the Pullman Palace Car Company. The engine burned what was then largely a refinery waste product called gasoline. Patton's first car had a mechanical transmission. Electric transmissions came later.

Patton and Pullman placed a number of electric cars in service. One was used by a contractor building a suburban railroad near Chicago. In this application, the Patton "locomotive" could handle five cars of rail and crossties. It's fair to conclude Patton's engine concept, modified and improved, led to other self-powered rail motor cars.

In 1895, at about the time Dr. Diesel was getting his diesel engine to run, the De La Vergne Refrigerating Machine Company of New York produced its first Model HA engine. The HA was a horizontal oil-burning, single-cylinder compression-ignition engine—a diesel—that would see considerable use in military applications, lighthouses, and factories without electricity.

De La Vergne went on to produce a line of larger and more powerful engines. In 1909, the reference to refrigeration disappeared from the company's name; De La Vergne was moving whole-hog into the engine business. Some historians regard the De La Vergne HA as the first compression-ignition diesel engine built in the United States.

Facing, EMD's origins: Early headquarters of the Electro-Motive Co. in Cleveland, presumably photographed after 1923 when "Engineering" was dropped from its name. *Photo Electro-Motive Division,* Trains *magazine, Kalmbach Media*

But at the time, there wasn't a diesel engine in production powerful enough to generate sufficient electricity to move railcars. In 1910, General Electric began looking for one that could. Richard McLean Dilworth, an itinerant machinist and electrician who worked for GE, teamed up with coworker and electrical genius Hermann Lemp, to put one together. Dick Dilworth will show up big-time later in our story.

One authority contends the world's first locomotive powered by a diesel engine came in 1913 from the innovations of Sulzer Brothers, the Swiss company that gave Rudolf Diesel his start. That effort had begun in 1909. The diesel prime mover was connected by jackshafts to two driving axles. To start the diesel, a small auxiliary engine would compress air with which to crank the main engine. The Sulzer locomotive ran in Switzerland and Germany, in one test faster than 60 miles an hour.

By 1913, most of the 240 railcars that GE and the McKeen Company had sold were sidelined due to mechanical difficulties and the soaring price of gasoline. But GE had success with what's commonly regarded as the first successful internal-combustion locomotive with an electric drive built in the United States. It went to the Minneapolis, St. Paul, Rochester & Dubuque Electric Traction Company in Minnesota, the "Dan Patch" line. This railroad had been conceived as an interurban, but it was never electrified. Its locomotive contained two 175-horsepower GE gasoline engines. By 1915, the Dan Patch had acquired three more locomotives like the first one. The original "Patch" still exists and is in the care of the Minnesota Transportation Museum in St. Paul.

After World War I, diesels began to mature and a sizable market in the rail industry developed. Overseas, Germany was building diesels for Russia, which had no factories of its own. These countries tested locomotives that used electrical, mechanical, hydraulic, and even pneumatic methods to transmit the power of a diesel engine to the running gear. In a pneumatic transmission, the diesel drove a compressor that pumped air into cylinders that were part of a running gear similar to that of a steam locomotive. In Scotland, the William Beardmore Company introduced a diesel engine to go into railcars on the London, Midland & Scottish and the Canadian National. Per horsepower the Beardmore engine weighed 20.5 pounds.

In the United States, De La Vergne would supply the Baldwin Locomotive Works with engines. McIntosh & Seymour would build engines for the American Locomotive Company. Winton, which was producing six-cylinder in-line diesels of up to 450 horsepower for stationary and marine use, was another candidate for the emerging locomotive market. Also on the list of manufacturers were Fairbanks-Morse; the Hooven, Owens, Rentschler Company; and Ingersoll-Rand.

Hamilton was aware that the government's push to pave rural roads to accommodate more automobiles was beginning to decimate the branch-line services in which one-size-fits-all trains had been operating in the years prior to World War I. He envisioned self-propelled, one-piece trains scampering at high speeds along secondary and branch lines, connecting with main-line passenger trains.

Electro-Motive and Winton embarked on a joint development effort to explore the market. Their first gas-electric car was delivered in July 1924 to the Chicago Great Western. The second car went to the Northern Pacific. Both contained 175-horsepower Winton Model 106 engines. Per foot of length, the cars weighed but 40 percent of earlier cars. Hamilton attempted to interest both GE and Westinghouse in his new car, but to no avail. Over time, Electro-Motive would sell around 500 of these self-propelled cars, some powered by gasoline, some by distillate, most with Winton engines.

Whatever Electro-Motive might later say, the Baldwin Locomotive Works produced the country's first dedicated freight diesel locomotive. Introduced on June 25, 1925, the prototypical No. 58501 developed 1,000 horsepower, more than did any other internal-combustion locomotive of the day. Used by Baldwin as an engineering test bed, the 58501 incorporated electric control features that gave it the equivalent of what later would be called the dynamic brake. It was designed specifically to pull freight trains.

The Pennsylvania Railroad and the Reading, both of which served Baldwin's plant at Eddystone, used No. 58501 for a time. The Reading used it to move coal trains over the 40 miles from Tamaqua to Reading, where it regularly handled 1,000 tons up the 0.7 percent grades at 16 miles an hour, 2,000-ton trains down the hills.

AN EARLY PROPONENT OF THE DIESEL-ELECTRIC

Samuel Vauclain, father of a compound steam locomotive that bore his name, was a Pennsylvanian and railroader all his life. He began his career as an apprentice in the machine shops of the Pennsylvania Railroad. In those days, machining was a manual job using hammers, chisels, and files. The grueling hours of forming metal permanently clenched Vauclain's hands but gave him a lifelong love of locomotives.

In his 20s, Vauclain joined the Baldwin Locomotive Works in Philadelphia; he became a shop foreman by age 27. He rose steadily through the ranks and moved with the company to its new, spacious facility in nearby Eddystone in the early 1900s. Vauclain became Baldwin's president in 1919.

The Baldwin Locomotive Works enjoyed a profitable business. The new plant at Eddystone could produce 10 steam locomotives a day. Though there was no financial incentive to rush into the fledgling diesel-electric business, President Vauclain had a perceptive mind. He was a contemporary of Rudolf Diesel and had watched the continuing evolution of the diesel engine. Vauclain believed in this modern technology. Publicly, he spoke many times about the possibilities of the diesel engine as a locomotive prime mover.

Vauclain claimed there was no purpose entering the diesel-electric market until specific parameters could be met. He foresaw a locomotive of at least 1,000 horsepower, in a weight range of less than 300 pounds per horsepower. Knowing the locomotive's initial cost would be high, not until Vauclain saw a commensurate increase in its thermal efficiency and a decrease in its cost of operation would he be tempted to build one.

He did, however, set his engineers to the task of designing a prototype locomotive that met his criteria. Thus, in June 1925, midway through Vauclain's tenure as president, Baldwin introduced its No. 58501. When Vauclain left the presidency in 1929, he remained on the company's board of directors until his death 11 years later, at age 84.

Samuel Vauclain (in locomotive cab). *Courtesy Hagley Museum and Library*

Above, The first practical internal-combustion locomotive with an electric drive, the "Dan Patch," in use at the Minnesota Transportation Museum in 1978. *Photo Frank E. Sandberg Jr.,* Trains *magazine, Kalmbach Media*

Facing, Rakish lines of an early McKeen car belied the mechanical problems inherent in its gas-electric design. *Photo Bill Kratville,* Trains *magazine, Kalmbach Media*

In the end, the rigors of such an assignment were too much for the 58501's diesel prime mover. It was withdrawn from test service and ultimately scrapped. But the locomotive made sufficient history that had its prime mover been sturdier, the Southern Pacific would have bought it.

Around the same time Baldwin entered the diesel competition, American Locomotive, GE, and Ingersoll-Rand together introduced a 300-horsepower box-cab demonstrator and five production copies. One of the locomotives went to the Central Railroad of New Jersey, which placed it in switching service in the Bronx on October 22, 1925. Since 1957, former CNJ 1000 has resided at the B&O Railroad Museum in Baltimore.

Even the Pennsylvania Railroad tried its hand at building diesel-electrics. In 1926, it turned out three switchers that were roughly the equivalent of its B1 electric locomotive. They contained prime movers from the Bessemer Gas Engine Company of Grove City, Pennsylvania. Years later, when dieselization of nearly all railroads was in full swing, the Pennsy made noises about how it might build its own road diesel-electrics at Altoona, but nothing consequential emerged.

The Boston & Maine came close to being an early and innovative American leader in the use of diesel-powered locomotives. In 1927, the Boston & Maine thought seriously about using German-made Krupp diesel-hydraulic power plants to ride atop 4-8-4 wheel arrangements. It ordered one, assigned it the road number 101, and took an option on 19 more. In December 1928, Krupp tested the 101 on the Prussian State Railways. The test flopped when the hydraulic transmission failed. The Boston & Maine canceled its order; the 101 never left Germany.

Canadian National's 1928 Beardmore-powered 9000 and 9001 are regarded by some as the first diesel-electrics designed for passenger service. By then, though, being first in the diesel locomotive race seemed to depend somewhat on the publicity.

Electro-Motive and Winton continued their efforts to persuade railroads to try a vehicle with which they could preserve, perhaps even expand, what branch-line business remained. Some successes resulted. As the program went on and horsepower went higher, the cars became more like locomotives, less like combinations of power car and revenue space.

Pioneering Central of New Jersey box-cab 1000 was born of three parents: American Locomotive, General Electric, and Ingersoll-Rand. Trains *magazine, Kalmbach Media*

One of Santa Fe's early "doodlebugs," the M.184, rumbles across the railroad's Pekin District in central Illinois in the late 1940s. *Photo Wallace W. Abbey, Center for Railroad Photography & Art Collection*

With Santa Fe sticking with heavy doodlebugs, Union Pacific showed the way in 1934 with its lightweight *M10000* streamliner. *Photo Union Pacific,* Trains *magazine, Kalmbach Media*

Considered the forerunner of the diesel, motor car M.190 poses with a 2-6-2 at the roundhouse in Ottawa, Kansas, in 1946. *Photo Wallace W. Abbey, Center for Railroad Photography & Art Collection*

Electro-Motive's own records indicate that its first standing-on-its-own-wheels locomotive was a 250-horsepower gas-electric switcher that was delivered to United Fruit Company for use in Central America.

In 1930, in a project that put it squarely into the locomotive business, Electro-Motive produced three box-cab locomotive-*cum*-baggage-car demonstrators. St. Louis Car Company built the bodies; 400-horsepower Winton Model 148 engines provided the power. The locomotives were less than 38 feet long, coupler face to coupler face. Electro-Motive later would call them its Model 60.

General Motors decided to take a stronger position in the markets for railroad equipment and lightweight internal-combustion engines both. In 1930, Kettering was investigating the thermal efficiency of the diesel engine when GM president Alfred Sloan asked for his thoughts. Boss Ket was to the point: "The trouble with the diesel is that manufacturers are trying to make a diesel like a steam engine. If folks would make a diesel the way it wants to be made, they might get somewhere."

Instead of the traditional four-cycle engine, Kettering started work on a two-cycle. He ordered a Winton engine with a unit injector and began experimenting. His results were promising enough that GM officials looked for facilities to manufacture an engine. Their hunt led to Winton's plant in Cleveland and a decision to acquire the engine maker. The transaction was finalized on June 20, 1930.

General Motors soon discovered that Winton's largest customer was Electro-Motive. There was much logic to acquiring not only the engine company but also its principal market. Hal Hamilton liked the proposal, and on the last day of 1930, Electro-Motive, too, became part of General Motors.

The alliance was fortuitous, especially for Electro-Motive, which badly needed what GM had in some abundance and it didn't: money. For some time, GM's Chevrolet Division covered Electro-Motive's payroll. Looking ahead, in 1937 Winton would become GM's Cleveland Diesel Division. In 1941, Electro-Motive Corporation would become GM's Electro-Motive Division.

With the growing interest by GM in diesel engines came a desire to carry the technology further. Winton of course had the experience and facilities with which to build diesel engines. So, GM Research and Winton's Experimental Engineering Departments laid out a new joint program. Within it began the development of a much-improved two-stroke-cycle diesel engine using the patented, revolutionary unit injector.

The unit injector pressurized the fuel within the injector instead of in a common fuel pump, as had been the usual practice. The injector was a metering device: per cycle, it delivered into the cylinder up to 475 cubic millimeters of fuel at a pressure of 5,500 to 6,000 pounds per square inch.

This first attempt at a two-cycle engine taught Winton and GM Research more about what didn't work than about what did. Winton built two single-cylinder test engines of a new design that could be operated—or so the test engineers had hoped—in either four-cycle or two-cycle mode. One of the engines went to Research in Detroit; the other stayed at Winton in Cleveland.

After both were run in four-cycle mode to establish their baseline performances, Research converted its engine to two-cycle. Then the problems began to show up. Camshafts and valve gear wouldn't run at the speeds a two-cycle engine required. There wasn't enough room in the cylinder head for the injector, so the head had to be redesigned. After the report card on the test engines was filled in, it was clear that Research designers would be staying after school. Winton never converted its test engine to two-cycle mode.

A third test engine, a single-cylinder two-stroke-cycle, was the result. There was still a lot of work to do on both the engine and the injector, but the idea of producing an eight-cylinder engine of 600 horsepower now was very much in the picture. At the time, the best existing eight-cylinder four-cycle engine would put out just 400 horsepower.

Facing, Charles Kettering (left) and Harold Hamilton pose in front of the Burlington's *Pioneer Zephyr* of 1934. Trains magazine, Kalmbach Media

The basics of this new diesel engine, the Model 201, fell into place in that third single-cylinder engine and in subsequent pre-production prototypes. At one point in 1932, five single-cylinder Model 201 engines and one six-cylinder engine were hammering away on test stands in Cleveland and Detroit.

GM was getting closer to having a decent engine that would power a decent locomotive.

—⁂—

As testing continued on the Model 201, Electro-Motive and Winton unveiled their largest propelled car, Santa Fe's articulated M.190. It developed 900 horsepower in its one-of-a-kind Model 12-194 distillate engine. Spark-ignited, the 194 was a biggie, yet it weighed only 20 pounds per horsepower, the limit Kettering believed a diesel engine had to observe before it would be suitable for a locomotive.

One wonders what might have become of the Santa Fe's passenger service had it valued its 1932 M.190 as the Burlington regarded its 1934 *Zephyr* and the Union Pacific its 1934 *M-10000*—that is, as equipment designed to minimize the cost of light-density lines and perhaps even generate new business on them.

The M.190, nicknamed the "doodlebug," was capable of high speeds, its engine half again as powerful as were the engines of its competitors' streamliners. It was as powerful as it was because Santa Fe had wanted an internal-combustion device that could manage a fair string of freight cars, and, later on, some experimental passenger service.

The Santa Fe seemed to appreciate the M.190, as it did all its propelled cars, for its reduced operating costs. But the railroad was skeptical enough about the M.190 that it made Electro-Motive guarantee it. Of course, Electro-Motive's service policies were better than are automobile manufacturers' guarantees even today. If you like the car, send us the money. If you don't like the car, send it back. The Santa Fe liked it, but not that much.

So much, then, for a forerunner to the *Super Chief*! Still, the M.190 was a step in the direction toward the fully viable diesel-electric locomotive. It represented the Santa Fe's most telling attack yet by an internal-combustion railcar on the dominance of steam. And it better prepared the Santa Fe for its upcoming alliance with General Motors.

MEET ME AT THE FAIR

Ralph Budd, president of the Burlington, was looking for a fresh way to boost passenger service and lower costs. Interested in Electro-Motive's upcoming internal-combustion engine, he visited Hal Hamilton at Cleveland's Winton plant. Hamilton showed Budd two eight-cylinder diesel engines under construction for the 1933–1934 Century of Progress World's Fair in Chicago.

Budd's next stop was the Detroit office of inventor Charles Kettering.

"We wouldn't dare sell you this thing," Kettering said. "We don't even know if it will run."

With that, Kettering invited Budd to observe the engines in action at the fair. He did, and he saw a stream of repairmen using a limitless supply of water from Lake Michigan to keep the engines running.

Budd looked to Hamilton, who also stood in the exhibit building, for reassurance. He got little. Hamilton estimated these first diesels would have a cylinder life of only 80,000 miles, and most of the other parts would wear out as quickly.

Dick Dilworth happened to be nearby, and Budd turned to him for a reaction. "What do you think of it?"

"She ain't much now," Dilworth said, "but she has hopes."

Believing General Motors would stay committed to the new diesel until it performed well, Budd went ahead with his order for a 600-horsepower Model 201A for the upcoming *Pioneer Zephyr*. Orders from the Union Pacific and Burlington weren't far behind.

Eugene Kettering, who had joined Winton three years earlier as "a very green kid just out of school," later added his perspective: "Before the eight-cylinders had been run, some brave soul decided it would be great to have them furnish power for the General Motors building at the fair. To mention the parts with which we had trouble in Chicago would take far too much time.

It was no fun, but we learned fast and a new design study was soon under way at Winton."

With a lot of help, the engines ran through both years of the fair. During these Depression times, the public and the railroad industry alike saw the new diesel as a hopeful sign of progress.

FIVE FINALLY, A LOCOMOTIVE PRIME MOVER

The Birth of the Legendary 567 Engine

JUST WHO SUGGESTED THAT WINTON'S UNTESTED MODEL 201 engines should power the General Motors exhibit at the Century of Progress Exhibition, commonly called the World's Fair, in Chicago in 1933 and 1934? Whomever it was appears to be a name lost in, if not buried beneath, GM's history. The eight-cylinder prototype hadn't even been fired up when the decision was made to use the first two production engines at the fair. While the engines looked good and they powered a Chevrolet assembly line all day long, they were infested with bugs. Maintenance crews lived in the basement of the exhibit building. A steady stream of replacement parts flowed from Cleveland to Chicago.

How bad were the 201's problems? Eugene Kettering, son of Boss Ket and at the time head of Winton's Experimental Engine Department, had overseen its development. He said in a speech years later that he didn't recall any problems with the dipstick.

The World's Fair 201s were "straight eights." An engine that Winton sent to the US Navy's test facility at Annapolis was a "straight 12." These were the only production 201s built, discounting two "straight sixes" and five or more single-cylinder test engines that never left Cleveland and Detroit.

A much-improved engine, the 201A, came along next. Eight-cylinder versions went into the Burlington's first *Zephyr*; its three siblings; and its cousin, the Boston & Maine's *Flying Yankee*. Winton was also working on a 16-cylinder version.

Up to this time, GM's diesels had evolved without great attention to standardization. Winton was supplying three versions, each with the blowers, water pumps, and other accessories needed for specific applications. The eight- and 16-cylinder 201As, for example, were headed for navy submarines.

Here and later, the navy's requirements limited the engines for railroad service. The V-16 201A weighed what the navy wanted it to weigh, which was less than it needed to weigh on the rails. It was more compact than it needed to be to fit into a locomotive.

Accordingly, and with an eye on the growing potential of the market, GM began designing an engine for railroad use, centering the work within Electro-Motive. The new engine would eliminate problems inherent in the 201A, such as the too-short lives of its components. Even as Winton introduced the 201A's successor, the 184, to the navy in 1936, GM was leveraging its experience to build an engine specifically designed to sit inside a locomotive car body and pull a train. When introduced by Electro-Motive in October 1938, the engine would be known as the 567.

Electro-Motive needed new digs. It had known for some time it would have to expand its factory to meet the demands for its locomotives, and possibly so it could manufacture under one roof all the major mechanical and electrical components of its

Facing, In a 1936 photo, the EMC factory floor mostly is crammed with switchers but also Union Pacific's new *City of Portland* streamliner (foreground) and Baltimore & Ohio 50 in the background. *Photo Electro-Motive Division,* Trains *magazine, Kalmbach Media*

The early eight-cylinder Winton 201A engine was problematic, but it helped make EMC competitive in the railroad business. *Photo Electro-Motive Division,* Trains *magazine, Kalmbach Media*

products. Electro-Motive almost acquired a site in Markham, south of Chicago, under which ran a subterranean river that was discovered just in time. Instead, the GM subsidiary bought 74 acres in McCook, about 18 miles southwest of downtown Chicago, from the Indiana Harbor Belt. Construction of the new plant, which would be known as La Grange for its mailing address—McCook did not have its own post office—began on March 27, 1935.

Phase one of construction was completed by late fall. In concept an assembly plant, not yet a manufacturing plant, the factory was equipped and ready for full production by April 1936.

The first domestic locomotive out of the new plant was a 600-horsepower switcher, No. 2301, with a 201A engine. It went to the Santa Fe on May 20, 1936. The 2301 hadn't been Santa Fe's first diesel, however. That honor had gone to a switcher out of American Locomotive, joining Santa Fe's roster back in February 1935.

Switchers were one thing; Electro-Motive built 50 of them largely on speculation. Railroads liked the short lead time to delivery, even though they didn't have the chance to doll the locomotives up their favorite way. But at least since 1935 Electro-Motive had been thinking well beyond switchers, toward the

EMC's demonstrator 511 has arrived from St. Paul at Chicago Union Station on Burlington's *Afternoon Zephyr* on September 28, 1936. *Photo Louis A. Marre Collection,* Trains *magazine, Kalmbach Media*

kind of powerful diesel-electric locomotive needed for rigorous over-the-road service.

Even as the 567 was working its way from drawing board to production, Electro-Motive was working on a locomotive that could develop 1,800 horsepower in two 12-cylinder V-type 201A engines. It would ride on two four-wheel, two-motor trucks. Electro-Motive's chief engineer, Dick Dilworth, had specified that it be the equal of a modern 4-6-4 steam locomotive, such as the New York Central's J-1, the Burlington's S-4, or the Milwaukee Road's F7.

Put it in a plain wrapper, Dilworth had instructed, a typical comment from a man who worked with a carpenter's pencil and a fat roll of butcher paper. To hear him talk about how a locomotive should look, he must have thought the boxcar was the most beautiful engineering achievement in railroading.

The first two examples of this new locomotive, EMC's E series, became test units and demonstrators. Electro-Motive had GE build the car bodies on welded underframes at Erie. When completed in 1935, the units received EMC road numbers 511 and 512, which were their construction numbers. While they weren't deemed specifically to be passenger train power, they probably were used that way most often. Moreover, they personified to a fault Dilworth's notion of styling. They had none.

In August 1935, the Baltimore & Ohio took delivery of virtually identical units. That same month the Santa Fe received its 1A and 1B, the same machinery inside considerably more stylish car bodies built by St. Louis Car Company on cast-steel underframes.

Electro-Motive's 511 and 512 served diligently, but not well. Not only did their design not lend itself to mass production but it was far from bug-free. Problems became apparent immediately after the locomotives were placed into service. In cold weather, air taken from the front end of the locomotive blew directly into the power plant, froze the radiators, and made it almost impossible for the crew to stay inside. The air passed through the engine room carrying snow, rain, and dirt. There was no way to filter the lubricating oil. The pumps, cooling systems, and steam generators had insufficient capacities, issues that were pronounced as the locomotive crossed the desert. The traction motors, when they weren't overheated, could neither handle heavy trains nor eliminate helper service.

Since the Santa Fe's 1A and 1B were essentially the same locomotive gussied up with a fancier exterior, they suffered the same shortcomings, failures, and breakdowns.

Seating was also a problem. The engineer and anyone else in the cab were too close to track level. Accounts began to come in of a sort of hypnosis from the blur of the crossties. It became clear the engine crew needed to be better protected. Accordingly, the operating cabs on production locomotives would be behind automobile-type windshields, above and back of sturdy framing members and smoothly tapered noses that would deflect cows and other unwelcome diversions. Boxcar construction of the body wasn't possible because of the cab, so the car body framework was similar to a Howe truss bridge.

Electro-Motive and the Santa Fe regarded their first diesel locomotives as laboratories on wheels. The generally unsatisfactory early experiences became the foundation of and the forerunner to the modern diesel-electric locomotive. Electro-Motive road diesels, first passenger and then freight, soon would be traveling the Trail of Holy Faith.

The first buildings at La Grange gave Electro-Motive 200,000 square feet of space in which to house about 350 people. By 1939, the working population would be 2,000. That number more than doubled by Pearl Harbor Day. By 1944, Electro-Motive employed 9,000. The La Grange facilities almost always were being expanded.

Electro-Motive would develop and build the 567 in its new La Grange plant. The design work began in the fall of 1936 and would take two years. Designs in 6-, 8-, 12-, and 16-cylinder sizes called for virtually no variation in components save for the crankcases and crankshafts. Most parts would fit any engine.

The 567 was a two-stroke-cycle compression-ignition engine, each piston of which displaced 567.5 cubic inches of air, hence the engine's model number. The cylinders were eight and a half inches in diameter; the pistons had a 10-inch stroke. The pistons compressed the air in the cylinders in a 16:1 ratio. Per horsepower, the 567 engine weighed a mere 17.9 pounds. Under standard conditions—temperatures 60 degrees Fahrenheit, altitude

With Dearborn Station as their backdrop, Santa Fe employees gather in front of the new 1B diesel-electric in 1935. *Photo Santa Fe Railway, Wallace W. Abbey Collection*

The "prime" of prime movers: EMC's revolutionary 567 diesel on the factory floor at La Grange. *Photo Electro-Motive Division, Wallace W. Abbey Collection*

Four EMC employees complete the assembly of a 16-567 engine for Santa Fe's order of FT diesels. *Photo Santa Fe Railway,* Trains *magazine, Kalmbach Media*

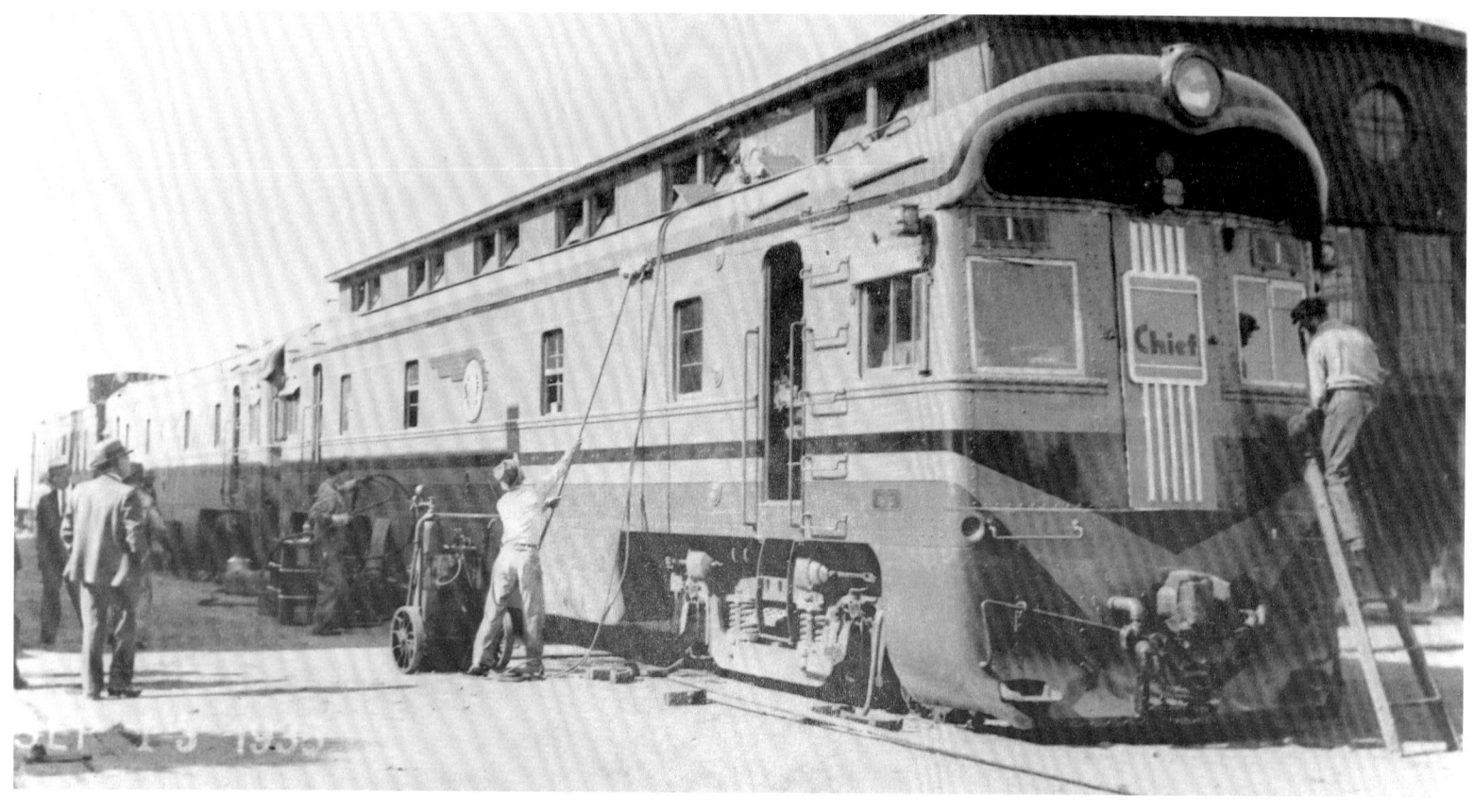

Above, Employees clean the 1A and 1B at San Bernardino in 1935; note the dynamometer car immediately behind the diesels. *Everette Lee DeGolyer Jr. Collection of US Railroad Photographs, DeGolyer Library, Southern Methodist University*

Facing, On its first run in 1935 with the new *Super Chief,* the 1A and 1B encounter a throng of onlookers at Pasadena. *Photo Santa Fe Railway, Wallace W. Abbey Collection*

1,000 feet—the 567 would produce 106 horsepower per cylinder. Every minute, the explosions in the cylinders would drop on the pistons a load equal to the weight of a navy heavy cruiser.

Early versions of the 567 were virtually identical except for the number of cylinders: two V-12s in a passenger locomotive, a V-6 or a V-12 in a switcher. Later, some switching locomotives would house a V-8. But once aboard the FT, the 16-cylinder 567 would be the last version of the engine to be developed.

For a big engine, the 567 would be easy to maintain: take off the top deck covers and most everything that might need to be unbolted or adjusted was right in front of the mechanic. Power assemblies—cylinder liners, pistons, connecting rods, cylinder heads, injectors—could be removed with a small block and tackle. Or just the piston and "conn rod" could be lifted out.

During these same days, Electro-Motive was advancing another technology: welding. To date, the conventional way to construct the frame of a locomotive was to cast it in steel. Most railroaders were ardently opposed to welding. Welded-steel underframes were lighter and stronger but, in the mid-1930s, to weld was simply too revolutionary for the railroads. In collaboration with Luken Steel's Lukenweld Division, Electro-Motive would

develop techniques that resulted in welded crankcases and even in welded locomotive frames, changing many minds about the technology. To make its point, Electro-Motive insisted the frameworks of its new La Grange buildings be welded together.

In 1937, the locomotive-assembly bay at La Grange was doubled in length to 1,000 feet, and manufacturing facilities were constructed for engines, generators, and more. No longer would La Grange be merely an assembly plant; now it was headed deeply into manufacturing. Since the summer of 1936, GM's Delco Products Division in Dayton had been working on designs for generators, controls, and traction motors. The first electrical components manufactured at La Grange would be ready in July 1938, right around the time the 567 was in production.

Santa Fe's diesel locomotives, beginning with those in passenger service, would show the touch of a professional industrial designer. The first locomotive to wear the railroad's inspired red, yellow, silver, and black styling—later to become known unofficially as the Warbonnet—went to work on the lightweight *Super Chief* on June 15, 1937.

Nine days later, a US patent was issued to Electro-Motive for the styling treatment; it would protect the Warbonnet design

New E1 diesels resplendent in the Warbonnet paint scheme pose with "Blue Goose" 4-6-4 No. 3460 at the 21st Street terminal in Chicago in 1938. *Photo Santa Fe Railway, Wallace W. Abbey Collection*

for 14 years. The patent was credited to William D. Otter, Hal Hamilton, Dick Dilworth, and Martin Blomberg, all of Electro-Motive, and Leland A. Knickerbocker and Chris J. Klein, design specialists for GM at Detroit.

On the same day, June 24, 1937, a second patent was issued largely to the same men. Assigned to GM, this patent protected the design of the E1 car body that the Santa Fe saw in its 201A-powered passenger diesels.

Between June 1937 and April 1938, the Santa Fe received 11 1,800-horsepower E1s, still powered by the 201A. Eight had operating cabs; three did not. By the spring of 1938, these locomotives, which constituted the 2 class, were handling the once-a-week *Super Chief* and *El Capitan* between Chicago and Los Angeles; the daily *San Diegan*; the daily Oakland–Bakersfield *Golden Gate*; and the daily *Kansas Cityan* and *Chicagoan* between Chicago and Wichita. One was assigned to the new *Tulsan* between Kansas City and Tulsa when that train was inaugurated on December 10, 1939.

Helping out on some of these assignments were the original passenger diesels, the 1A and 1B, which by then had become the 1 and the 10, modified with elevated cabs and three-axle trucks in which the leading axle was the idler. Dilworth had championed that arrangement for some time. After that, it would be 17 months before the passenger diesel fleet would again begin to grow, with the introduction of a 2,000-horsepower unit. In that time the elevated cab would come off the 10 and it would become a booster unit, the 1A.

Electro-Motive would call its new entrant the *Streamliner*, even unto its final versions. Its more common designation, depending on details, was E3, E4, E5, or E6.

When the *Streamliner* brought the 567 engine to Santa Fe passenger service in the E6, it rode on the same type of three-axle, two-motor trucks that had been under the 201A-powered E1s. Numbered 11–15, with booster units for the 11, 12, 13, and 15, the E6s bumped the E1s off the *Super* and *El Cap*. The order for the 14's booster had been canceled.

Purists will insist the 11 and 11A were E3s, not E6s. True, the E6s did have an air-operated retractable coupler behind the pilot and the 11 didn't. But the 11 and 11A weren't different enough from the rest of the series to warrant a Santa Fe class of their own.

Through the years, Electro-Motive would recall how an E unit, sold to the Seaboard Air Line in October 1938, was the first out of its plant to contain La Grange–manufactured 567 engines and electrical transmissions. This unit, which carried Electro-Motive serial number 832, was part of the first of three three-unit E4 consists for the *Orange Blossom Special*, the Seaboard's premium streamliner between Washington, DC, and Florida. The conventional wisdom about it would be valid were it not for an E4 with the Electro-Motive serial number, and road number, 822.

Electro-Motive didn't talk much about the 822, which was essentially an engineering test bed. The frame of serial 822 had been laid down at Electro-Motive in August 1938, at approximately the same time as were the frames of the Seaboard locomotives. The plan had been to rate the Seaboard units at 1,800 horsepower each, pending tests with the 822.

The 822 was officially released in September 1938. It was sent off to run on the Burlington, where it pedaled back and forth between Chicago and Galesburg. Its performance merited a new rating: 2,000 horsepower. While the Burlington tests of the 822 were underway, the first of the Seaboard's E4s was assembled, painted, and set aside to await the arrival of automatic train control and other accessories specified by the railroad.

So, while the Seaboard units may have been the first altogether commercial Es out of La Grange to contain the 567 engine and La Grange–built generators and motors, the first such locomotive to pull a train was Electro-Motive's prototype 822. Until it was sold to the Kansas City Southern on July 31, 1939, the 822 served Electro-Motive as a test unit and demonstrator. The first three Seaboard E4s would also serve in this capacity, in a convincing way that doubtless helped sell some Model Fs.

In fact, the 567, the first built-for-a-locomotive prime mover out of General Motors, would, upon its arrival in quantity, doom the steam locomotive.

Ready to barnstorm the country, the first FT emerges from the La Grange factory in its distinctive olive, black, and gold livery.
Photo Electro-Motive Division, Wallace W. Abbey Collection

SIX THE MODEL F STANDARD

In the End, Electro-Motive Had to Prove It Could Handle Freight

QUITE LIKELY, THE CONCEPT OF A LOCOMOTIVE DESIGNED specifically for freight service was as old at Electro-Motive as was the idea of the *Streamliners*. Probably, it was as old as was the concept that generated the box-cab 511 and 512. In one piece of GM literature, 1933 pops up as the year in which Electro-Motive conceived the freight diesel.

Electro-Motive was in the business of building and selling engines and locomotives. However large was the market for passenger diesels, the market for freight diesels was many times larger. But at the time it acknowledged the potential for a freight locomotive, Electro-Motive hadn't been in a position to meet *any* market for such a machine. Among other things, it had needed a bigger and better diesel prime mover than the 201A.

Now, the 567 engine had been introduced. La Grange could build both engines and electrical components under its roof. Now, Electro-Motive could turn its attention to a new principal product.

Building a diesel-electric locomotive to pull freight trains wasn't really the revolutionary technological excursion some have called it. When it was still the Electro-Motive Corporation, yet to become GM's Electro-Motive Division, it simply took the next logical step in the long engineering walk away from steam, based on the experience gained with its earlier models.

Speaking to the Pacific Railway Club in May 1949, Hal Hamilton mapped out the progression of the freight diesel:

By the end of the '30s, we had pretty well proven that the diesel locomotive was effective as far as switch-engine operations were concerned, and as a passenger locomotive, and then we undertook to build a diesel locomotive for freight service. This appeared to be a big job, and whether or not we would be successful was a guessing contest. We finally worked ourselves up to the state of mind where we were willing to spend half a million, and another three hundred thousand to test the locomotive we were going to spend half a million to build. We built the locomotive and turned it over to the railroads for them to test.

Just how big was the job? Surprisingly, Hamilton said, it wasn't as big as Electro-Motive had told itself it would be. While handling freight trains was different from handling passenger trains, not as much diesel horsepower would be required as was first thought. The nature of the steam locomotive had made pulling freight trains a more complicated task than it had to be.

Moreover, even before its deservedly famous olive-and-gold 5,400-horsepower 103 would undertake its nationwide exposure, Electro-Motive had already seen what some of its earlier locomotives, even those not designed for the service, could do with freight trains.

Milton Gardner, at the time a field service representative for and later general sales manager of Electro-Motive, was at Lincoln, Nebraska, one day doctoring chisel-nosed Burlington

E1 diesels 8 and 5 approach San Diego with train 74, the southbound *San Diegan*, on August 2, 1947. *Photo Stan Kistler*

Zephyr locomotives when the 511 and 512 led a long passenger train into town. Some of Gardner's associates were aboard.

He asked, "Where have you guys been?"

"Oh," they said, "we've been down in southern Illinois, pulling coal trains."

"Amos 'n Andy," "Mutt and Jeff," or whatever one wishes to remember as their nicknames, the first diesels for Santa Fe's *Super Chief* had come out of the factories to find themselves in the same shakedown service: southern Illinois coal.

Well and good. Somehow the idea of those box-cabs on a freight train doesn't seem far-fetched. But to assign to freight service a graceful and fleet-footed trio of E4s decorated for the *Orange Blossom Special*? How far-fetched was *that*?

On Tuesday, October 25, 1938, Seaboard cab units 3000 and 3001, with booster unit 3100 between them, were moved out of La Grange and over the Baltimore & Ohio Chicago Terminal (B&OCT) to B&O's Lincoln Street Yard. At 7:00 a.m. on Wednesday, October 26, the 6,000-horsepower locomotive was due to start out for Washington, DC, where the following Monday it would be delivered to its new owner.

Electro-Motive was buying the fuel and the lubricating oil. It secured insurance to cover the value of the locomotive, since the B&O wouldn't assume responsibility for it. The Seaboard units would see their first revenue service in a road freight test sponsored by EMC.

Gardner was aboard out of Chicago. Through the night the Es trundled eastward, leading a consist the details of which are forgotten except that it was freight. In the morning, the train was 10 hours ahead of the B&O's freight schedule. Through the second day the Es galloped toward Washington and the northern end of the Seaboard. When they arrived, they'd clipped off another 10 hours.

Could diesels pull freight trains? Electro-Motive knew they could long before the railroads were ready to listen to the idea— and well before Electro-Motive itself had come up with a product designed specifically for the job.

―――

Electro-Motive's freight locomotive began to take tangible form on February 1, 1939. An internal engineering release issued that day got the project going:

This release file is being set up to enable the Engineering Department to release drawings for the construction of a 2,700-horsepower freight locomotive. This locomotive will be known as Model "F" and will consist of two sections: section No. 1 (front) and section No. 2 (rear). Each release will specify under "section" that section of the locomotive to which the release applies. It is, however, essential that the locomotive be regarded as a complete unit made up of two sections and not as two separate units, particularly since neither section can be operated without the other. Each section will have one 16-567 engine and two four-wheel trucks.

Each section's engine, then, would draw 1,350 horsepower; thus, the inference to Freight Thirteen suggested by the locomotive's name: FT.

This locomotive would be known within Electro-Motive as the Model F Standard. There would be variations, as we'll see, beginning with the first commercial order.

Two Model Fs coupled back-to-back would stretch 193 feet between the pulling faces of their couplers. Each two-section Model F would draw 2,700 horsepower from its pair of 16-cylinder 567 engines. Its two 600-volt direct-current D8 main generators would power eight D7 traction motors. A belt-driven auxiliary generator would sit atop each main generator to provide direct current to charge the batteries. The generators and motors would be Electro-Motive products designed at GM's Delco subsidiary, similar to General Electric components of roughly the same capacities. Allis-Chalmers would provide some of the electrical control mechanisms, Woodward the engine governors, Gardner-Denver the air compressors, and Harrison the oil coolers and radiators.

The electrical controls would be so arranged that the main generators would pump out maximum voltage no matter in which of its eight positions the engineer's throttle was placed. Thus, at low speeds the locomotive would be incredibly powerful compared to anything the railroad world had yet seen, save for GM's E-type passenger engines, which were using the same system.

To call the freight locomotive a General Motors product rather than an Electro-Motive product was entirely justified. If the practice begun with passenger diesels was carried over to the

Above, Three Seaboard Air Line E6s, the first equipped with the new 567 diesel, pose at an unidentified roundhouse in 1938. *Photo Electro-Motive Division, Wallace W. Abbey Collection*

Facing, Uniformed EMC employees at La Grange wind electrical parts for the FT's main generators. *Photo Electro-Motive Division, Wallace W. Abbey Collection*

Model F, the crank handles on the cab windows were those used in some GM automobiles of the day.

In order to use the full capabilities of the electrical transmission, the traction motors of the Model F could be connected in series, in series and parallel simultaneously, or in parallel only. Using an automotive comparison, the electrical transmission provided the equivalent of a low gear, a high gear, and overdrive.

In the experimental 103, the transition in the motor connections was in part automatic. In production Model Fs, the engineer, watching an ammeter, would handle the transition himself.

Aboard each locomotive, optionally, would be a small steam generator designed not to heat or cool a passenger train but to keep the locomotive warm in freezing weather. The steam generator's water tank held but 300 gallons. The experimental 103 would have full-size steam generators built in.

A variety of traction-motor-to-axle-gear ratios would be available, each with its own range of tractive effort, each with its own

Facing, The FT's dynamic brake cooling assembly, upside down on the shop floor. The center motor drives the two rooftop exhaust fans. *Photo Electro-Motive Division, Wallace W. Abbey Collection*

Above, An FT two-axle Blomberg truck, shown with one of the two traction motors installed. *Photo Electro-Motive Division, Wallace W. Abbey Collection*

maximum speed. The gear ratio was critical: spin the traction motors' armatures too rapidly and the banding wires that held the motors together would break and the motors would fly apart.

When the 103 was tested on the Santa Fe, the pinions on the motor shafts would have 18 teeth, the spur gears on the axles 59. The 59:18 combination would give the 103 a top safe speed of 73 miles an hour.

All added up, the 5,400-horsepower 103 would weigh 910,200 pounds. It would generate about 220,000 pounds of tractive effort.

Like that of the earlier E units, the car body of each section was a modified Howe truss. The body panels weren't included in the stress calculations on the framing; they added nothing to the strength of the structure. They were of three-eighths-inch plywood laminated to galvanized steel, with the edges sealed. They "floated," held in place by battens but not rigidly fastened to the framing. Car body design would follow Electro-Motive's "covered wagon" styling, as the streamlined freighters had come to be known, although the nose would be blunter. Some of the jigs and fixtures used to shape the nose sections of the Es and

Facing, Rooftop cooling fans, designed to draw air in through the car body grilles, across the radiators, then out the roof. *Photo Electro-Motive Division, Wallace W. Abbey Collection*

Below, Engineer's control stand on the original FT; note the absence in this 1939 photo of dynamic braking controls, added later. *Photo Electro-Motive Division, Wallace W. Abbey Collection*

Facing, Ready for its compound curves: Electro-Motive welders assemble the nose structure of an FT. *Photo Electro-Motive Division, Wallace W. Abbey Collection*

Above, With dynamometer car and two passenger cars trailing, demonstrator 103 pauses at Burnham in Denver on the Denver & Rio Grande Western on May 16, 1940. *Photo Otto C. Perry, Western History Collection, The Denver Public Library*

The 103 on its demonstration run, hauling a passenger train somewhere on the Northern Pacific early in 1940. *Photo Electro-Motive Division, Wallace W. Abbey Collection*

the Rock Island's similar TA diesels would be used again on the Model Fs.

Inside, the Model F would be finished in suede gray DuPont Dulux enamel trimmed in black. Outside, the locomotive would be treated to a six-step process of priming, sanding, and glazing, and then to 7 to 10 coats of DuPont Duco lacquer according to the customer's design specifications. The exterior colors of the experimental 103 were perhaps best described as something approaching Pullman green, similar to olive, along with black and DuPont's imitation gold.

At first, the two two-section locomotives carried as road numbers the construction or serial numbers of their cab sections, 1030 and 1031. But likely, Electro-Motive was advised by westerners familiar with railroad labor agreements that in the two numbers could lie much difficulty. By the time it was ready to be introduced to the world, the demonstrator carried only one road number, 103. Individually, the four sections were identified by their serial numbers, modestly and not where the numbers could readily be seen.

On its test runs, the cab section with serial number 1031 was always in the lead. Quite possibly the 1030 had had a steam line run through its pilot to heat the dynamometer car and thus had to trail. Or perhaps automatic train control equipment had been installed only in serial 1031.

Thus far, in a broad sense, the new freight locomotive followed the general features of its predecessor *Streamliner* passenger version. But there the similarity ended.

The length and weight of the freight diesel's 16-cylinder 567 prime movers, each of which in horsepower was a *Streamliner* engine and a third, dictated that the car body be in two sections. The design called for all the locomotive's weight to be on powered axles, four of them per section, to maintain the proper weight on drivers. Each section would be considerably shorter than was an E unit. The A and B sections would be of slightly different lengths. They would be joined by a massive forged drawbar that was just under the car body floor, well above standard coupler height. The drawbar—or, as it was often called, the link—terminated under each section in a huge ball joint. Once fastened together, the two sections of a Model F weren't going to come apart except in a backshop.

The trucks under each section would be asymmetrically positioned, possibly for reasons of weight distribution and certainly to make room at the cab end of the A section and at the rear of the B section for National Malleable M-380 rubber draft gear and AAR type E couplers on special extra-heavy shanks. A standard coupler, by which a Model F could be attached to the rest of the railroad world, would exist only in the nose of the A section and at the rear of the B section.

As if that weren't enough to confound railroads that operated independent two-unit or three-unit passenger diesels, for yet another reason the two sections of a Model F had to stay together: all the batteries were in the A section. Absent the A section, the B section had no low-voltage control current. Absent the B section, the A section was almost an orphan that could only be coupled to a train backward.

Neither the A section nor the B section was completely enclosed. Instead of one or two doors, a simple canvas closure covered the opening between the two car bodies, above their connecting center drawbars. At the rear of the B section was a door and a full diaphragm.

If there were anything aboard the Model F that both Electro-Motive and its customers might wish had been something else, it would be the mechanisms that cooled the diesel engines. Cooling water circulated from the engines through radiators mounted inside along the sides of the car body, just under the roof. Shutters could be opened or closed manually to help control the temperature of the water. Four 34-inch fans in the roof were driven by shafts connected to extensions of the engines' crankshafts through right-angle drives and gear trains called "speed increasers." The fans would suck 80,000 cubic feet of air per minute per engine into the engine rooms through the radiators and propel it out through the roof.

The fans could create partial vacuums in the engine rooms. But on the experimental 103 there was no way to stop the fans. Consequently, in the winter the engine rooms could, and did, get cold enough to endanger the engine if it idled for long periods. Production locomotives would have a manually operated friction clutch in each fan's drive train. Adjusting the radiators and fan clutches would become work for the locomotive's fireman or, if there was one, the maintainer.

It was disputed whether Electro-Motive or the railroads designed the manual controls. But since the fireman had to be aboard under labor agreements, he ought to have work to do. So cooling controls that had been automatic in earlier locomotives were manual in the Model F.

Too, Electro-Motive was attempting to limit the parasitic load on the Model F's electrical transmissions. That's one reason why most accessories were powered by belt drives and not by electric motors. Also, in freight service, FTs would spend a lot of time going downhill in idle. Their engines wouldn't require, then, the same high-capacity cooling systems they'd need on the uphill pulls.

During a particularly contentious labor disagreement in later years, Santa Fe testified that had the railroad known its union would go after a requirement for a fireman in each unit, it would have required Electro-Motive to make automatic every function a fireman could perform.

By the time EMC began cutting and welding metal for its experimental 103, a world of work was behind it: theorizing, investigating, analyzing, and planning for the ultimate product. Dick Dilworth testified to this effort before a 1943 Presidential Emergency Board. He took the board back to the early history of Electro-Motive, before its switching and passenger locomotives were being built:

"Our development of the diesel locomotive required the blending of three controlling factors: physical limitations, engineering knowledge, and economics.

"It is natural that the economic factor should be controlling, for unless the finished product had a genuine economic justification the enterprise could not be a commercial success. The limitation factor included such things as track gauge, clearances, wheel loadings, safety laws, coupler heights, with the natural laws of adhesion being the principal one. [Engineering] knowledge covers the state of the art involved and the special knowledge we had acquired from many years of experience and research."

Once Electro-Motive had decided it had the engineering know-how, it confronted a major decision: What physical form should the locomotive take? Dilworth, again:

> As far back as 1912 or 1914, it was possible for any engineer with a slide rule, some optimism, and a pad of paper to sit down and figure out that if he could build a diesel locomotive it would be a worthwhile thing to do. But the trouble was that the diesel engine itself was so heavy and so large that by the time you got an engine with sufficient power to be useful as a locomotive you could not get wheels under it and you could not get it through the tunnels.
>
> It was not until a good many years had passed from the first idea of the diesel engine that several arts—not only having to do with engine-building but with the building of dynamos, electric machines, and cooling radiators—had been developed.

All of a sudden it was possible, Dilworth concluded, "to build a type of diesel locomotive that could be put together with some hope of success."

Electro-Motive undertook a lengthy study of wheel arrangements, taking into account wheel loadings relative to both track structure and adhesion. The study showed that while different forms of the locomotive could be correct from an engineering perspective, building the locomotive in units that could be "multipled" together offered the best operational mix of economy and utilization.

During the decades of steam, the locomotive was in near-constant development, providing the railroads a selection of sizes and power to fit the variety of its assignments, both road and yard. In contrast, Dilworth pointed out, dieselization would not offer so many options:

"It was plain to see, in introducing a new form of motive power, our economic factor would go out the window if we attempted to produce the sizes and types to match the variety of steam locomotives the railroads had at their command."

But, Dilworth added, "In the diesel we had one natural advantage not possessed by the conventional steam locomotive, and that was the possibility of multiple-unit operation and control.

"Extensive consultations with railway mechanical and operating people made it apparent that if we were wise enough to select initially the proper unit sizes, we could, by use of the multiple control idea, produce relatively few types of locomotives. By providing multiple control features, we could supply to the railroads a highly flexible type of motive power that would provide the optimum in general efficiency."

Here, Dilworth returned to his economic argument.

"The dominant factor in the entire project must of necessity be the economics. Therefore, the capital investment to be considered by the railroads, in substituting diesel power for steam, was of paramount importance. And volume production is the direct road to lower cost of a finished article. We therefore launched our diesel locomotive development around the philosophy of multiple control, permitting the operation of one or more units from one control station.

The original 103 demonstrator, now wearing the number 6100 for new owner Southern Railway, is ready for delivery at La Grange in 1941. *Photo Electro-Motive Division, Wallace W. Abbey Collection*

Two FTs and an F3 lead a westbound freight along Burlington's commuter district at West Hinsdale, Illinois, August 30, 1949. *Photo Wallace W. Abbey, Center for Railroad Photography & Art Collection*

"The selection of sizes and types of locomotives was our gamble. Subsequent experience seems to indicate we were reasonably correct."

Electro-Motive began to advance the idea that most railroads had taken the steam locomotive, in terms of size and weight, about as far as it could. Even though larger, heavier, and more powerful locomotives had been needed for years, they couldn't be built because they wouldn't fit on the railroad. EMC seemed to relegate the preceding 25 years of steam-locomotive development to the status of continuous experiments. It had a practical answer: diesel-electric units that could be coupled into consists with far more total power than even the largest steam locomotive could produce.

Did the railroads go along with this thinking?

Not totally. The Santa Fe, Electro-Motive's first and best potential customer, sent a management team armed with a large roll of drawings from its Mechanical Department to the new La Grange plant.

"Immediately we were precipitated into a situation," Dilworth testified, "which, if accepted, would destroy the basic concept of our design, manufacturing, and operating program. We were certain that standardization, once accepted and established, would be of inestimable future value to the railroads. We were unsuccessful with the Santa Fe, and after a few days the railroad officials wrapped up their bundle of drawings and left our plant without placing an order."

But, of course, the Santa Fe would be back.

In his labor testimony, Dilworth expanded on Electro-Motive's approach to basic locomotive design:

> Now, to pull so big a train up so much grade requires so much tractive effort, and so much tractive effort requires so much weight on drivers, and that is the first thing that has to be set down in the design of any locomotive.
>
> The weight on drivers, and therefore the number of drivers it is going to take to carry that weight, and the number of traction motors we are going to put on those drivers, are all determined before we take up the second part of the customer's specification, that is, the scheduled speed at which he wants to run. It is not until we come to talking about the scheduled speed that we give any consideration to horsepower at all. Our freight engine has got to weigh 164 pounds on drivers for every horsepower in the prime mover.

Standardization, Dilworth reiterated, was key:

> We want to build a locomotive as nearly as possible on the same basis as we build Chevrolets. We want to be able to manufacture and sell a locomotive off the shelf, so to speak. Here it is.
>
> We are considerably interested in the possibilities of quantity production. We want to be able to take care of 80 percent of the various operating jobs the customers present to us and take care of maybe 90 percent of the jobs with that same locomotive with minor modifications in design. Then we want to say, about the remaining 10 percent, well, let our competition take them, or get somebody to build you a tailor-made job for that one, or change your operating conditions so you can use the standardized locomotive.
>
> In order to approach that goal, we, some time ago, at the same time we were gambling on the size of the cylinders, and the size of the engine we were going to put in these locomotives, gambled on how much they were going to weigh.
>
> We said that a diesel freight engine, if it is going to be manufactured, ought to be about so big, and we set 2,700 rated horsepower; and then we said, referring to various steam locomotive types, this diesel has got to be a Mikado in the prairies, a Santa Fe in the foothills, and a little Mallet in the mountains.
>
> It has got to be, without modification in design, either a Mikado and a Santa Fe, or a Santa Fe and a Mallet, or, with such modifications as we can make, it has got to be a Mikado and a Mallet.

On November 3, 1939, the 103 stuck its nose outside Electro-Motive's back gate for the first time. Shrouded in its Plymetl-covered modified-Howe-truss car bodies, its 64 pistons pumped furiously. Its 40-inch driving wheels responded to the electrical pressure of 600 volts coming out of four main generators into 16 traction motors. The 103 was perhaps more an experiment than a demonstrator. Coupled to a few empty cars, it shuttled up and down the B&OCT for a time. Then it was taken back inside the plant for the inevitable troubleshooting and adjustments.

When the 103 next appeared, it would begin what history has been conditioned to appreciate as a nearly flawless nationwide tour of 83,764 miles in 35 states over the two dozen railroads that had in effect told EMC, "Sure, we'll see what your new locomotive will do, if you'll pay part of the cost."

The nationwide evaluation of the 103 in revenue freight service began on the Burlington on November 25, 1939. The locomotive made two round trips between Chicago and Kansas City and one round trip between Chicago and Denver. It did well. It was back in Chicago by December 20. Then it toured the West and the Midwest on the Santa Fe for more than a month; we'll look closely at these tests. In mid-1940, the 103 headed east; it was back at La Grange in October. The Southern Railway, impressed with its performance, would buy the 103 on May 26, 1941, and give it the road number 6100.

Time and again, the chronicles of this 11-month sojourn have been based on an Electro-Motive publication, *83,000 Miles: Now the Story Can Be Told*, published after completion of the nationwide tests. A fancier promotion piece for a locomotive probably couldn't be found. The large, hardbound, attractively boxed volume was targeted at railroad executives and others who could influence locomotive purchases. It contained much more information on how the 103 had performed in the field than had any other document made public.

But the thing is, *83,000 Miles* sometimes took indecent liberties with the facts.

To begin with, readers could assume it was a complete log of all the tests. It wasn't. It chronicled only some of the exploits of the 103 on no more than 16 railroads; Electro-Motive left the impression the 103 had visited 25 Class 1 properties. Only the subset of railroads the publication covered were represented on the frequently published map of the 103's demonstrations.

The *83,000 Miles* publication failed to record a trip over the Southern Pacific from Los Angeles up the San Joaquin Valley to Oakland. It neglected to mention that when the 103 reached Peoria from Minneapolis over the Minneapolis & St. Louis, at least by one local newspaper account, it did a turn east over the Pennsylvania Railroad to Valparaiso and back. Photographs show that after it had completed its freight service demonstrations, the 103 was brought back by the Santa Fe to test in passenger service between Chicago and Los Angeles.

It's doubtful we'll ever reconstruct the full exploits of the 103. The complete record seems lost. Moreover, some of the tests reported in *83,000 Miles* were not as they had been performed.

In the First Diesel Case, which we'll look at later, *83,000 Miles* was introduced into evidence. The publication had compared the 103 on the Santa Fe to that of a 5001-class 2-10-4 between Barstow and Bakersfield in terms of speed and availability, and it compared its fuel economy to the 5001 between Barstow and San Bernardino. At the time, the Santa Fe's 5000-class engines were considered the largest nonarticulated steam locomotives in the world. Figuratively wagging his finger at the copywriter to whom his office had provided complete details of the 103's tests, a Santa Fe official testified that the published diesel-to-steam comparisons had actually stacked the 103 up against an older, lighter, less powerful 3800-class 2-10-2.

Moreover, rather than average all the data for similar test runs, the copywriter had selected the individual runs that most favored the diesel. The publication dwelled on total time over the road, not actual running time, which skewed the comparison even more in favor of the diesel.

Besides, *83,000 Miles* had failed to mention that twice during its 11-month barnstorming tour, half or all of the 103 had been hauled back to La Grange for redesign and refit. Nor did the publication acknowledge the multitude of lesser problems that had cropped up around the 103 during the tests.

Highly effective as a sales tool, *83,000 Miles* fell decidedly short as a definitive engineering study.

Yet given all the literature's shortcomings and discrepancies, Electro-Motive's locomotive 103 was a hit. Its durability and eye-popping performance with heavy trains on the most demanding grades sold much of the industry on the idea that a diesel would work very well, indeed, in freight service.

Take it out and see how you like it, EMC had said. There was no cost or obligation, except the usual expense of running and maintaining any locomotive.

Most of the railroads that tried the Model F ordered some.

Two Chicago & North Western FTs and an F3 arrive at Kickapoo Tower, near Peoria, Illinois, to pick up a three-unit helper engine before climbing Radnor Hill. *Photo Wallace W. Abbey,* Trains *magazine, Kalmbach Media*

However much Electro-Motive wanted to sell a mass-produced freight locomotive that would be uniform across the railroad industry except for exterior paint, this was not to be.

The range of needs for diesel freight power was broader than could be met economically by a single 2,700-horsepower locomotive or by two 2,700-horsepower locomotives coupled back-to-back. In some applications, one two-section FT wasn't hefty enough to do the job, but two two-section FTs wasted horsepower and investment dollars. As designed, the Model F had no answer for a railroad that needed a horsepower rating between 2,700 and 5,400, say around 4,000.

Dilworth recognized this, calling the undividable sections of the Model F the biggest mistake of his career. In the 1954 biography, *The Dilworth Story*, author Franklin M. Reck relates that Dilworth wanted to correct his mistake quickly, but by then the United States was at war and the War Production Board had frozen locomotive designs, in part to minimize inventories of replacement parts. Not until the F2 came along in 1946 did EMD's freight diesel "sections" become independent "units," except on the Santa Fe and a few other roads. They, as we'll see, had ordered their locomotive components as free-standing, self-sufficient entities to begin with.

There was one way to resolve this problem of limited locomotive capacities. The Great Northern, Rock Island, Minneapolis & St. Louis, and Lackawanna took advantage of it. By adding a booster section with the drawbar of the original design at both ends, a permanently coupled 4,050-horsepower A-B-A configuration, later known as the FT-SB, was possible. Since the virtually empty and overhanging end of the B section was built largely to make room for a draft gear that wouldn't be there, the car body could be shortened by several feet.

The downside of the A-B-A was that if one section went belly-up, all three had to be pulled out of service. With a conventional FT, only two sections would need to go to the barn if one went bad—or, on the Santa Fe and to a limited extent elsewhere, just the one. Roads that had acquired conventional FTs might discover their diesel shops were full of perfectly good locomotives with the bad luck of being permanently attached to sections that were bad order.

In total, between 1939 and 1945, Electro-Motive constructed 1,098 sections of its Model F. Twenty-five railroads acquired the locomotive from the factory, if one counts two Southern Railway subsidiaries as separate companies. Because of Electro-Motive's war-related responsibilities, 500 of the locomotives came out of the plant in 1944.

So then, after Electro-Motive had sold out its Model F production, were there adherents to steam still standing proud?

There were many, including these major lines: the Pennsylvania Railroad, self-proclaimed "Standard Railroad of the World," and its close allies Wabash and Norfolk & Western; Union Pacific; Southern Pacific, but not SP's affiliated Cotton Belt; Texas & Pacific; Illinois Central; Nickel Plate; Chesapeake & Ohio; New Haven; Florida East Coast; a stretch, perhaps, but Canadian National and Canadian Pacific, and their stateside subsidiaries.

The absence of the Pennsy, UP, and SP from the roster of FT buyers suggests that before the revolution would be won, the resistance to the idea of diesels in freight service remained to be overcome by the descendants of the FT. Or by—*gasp!*—the products of other erecting floors than EMD's.

The Union Pacific would acquire the first three 2,000-horsepower Fairbanks-Morse "Erie-builts" for freight service in 1945, soon regeared for passenger service. The Pennsylvania would not acquire freight diesels until 1947, and it would spread its business around. The Southern Pacific would wait until, postwar, EMD had refined its 1,350-horsepower FT into the much-improved 1,500-horsepower F3 before it began to apply internal-combustion technology to a job historically the province of its articulated steam engines. Some other holdouts wouldn't begin their conversions until hood-unit road switchers became the functional equivalents of "covered wagons."

Clearly, the Model F had taught Electro-Motive how to build even better locomotives and how to continue to improve freight train handling, shorten schedules, and reduce operating costs. The FT had started a trend that, once underway, was irreversible.

Facing, The crew of the first westbound run of EMC 103 would have had this view of a steam-powered eastbound freight train near Ash Fork, Arizona. *Photo Jack Delano, Prints & Photographs Division, Library of Congress*

Dick Dilworth looks on as Santa Fe's John Morris takes the controls of the first FT. *Photo Santa Fe Railway,* Trains *magazine, Kalmbach Media*

SEVEN A MIKADO ON THE PRAIRIES, A MALLET IN THE MOUNTAINS

The 103 Goes to Work on the Santa Fe Trail

WHATEVER SORT OF PERFORMER ELECTRO-MOTIVE SAW ITS new Model F to be, the Santa Fe would give it an opportunity to show what it could do over a reasonable span of time and service. In December 1939, word spread around the Santa Fe that Electro-Motive's 103 was coming. Motive-power chief John Purcell circulated a letter quoting the railroad's contract with EMC: the railroad would supply, free of charge, the use of its tracks, shops, and other facilities, operating and running-maintenance labor, fuel, lubricating oil, and other supplies.

E. G. Sanders, the Santa Fe's fuel conservation engineer, then firmed up plans by which a 12,000-gallon tank car, AT&SF 100671, would be equipped at Topeka with hoses and connectors for diesel fuel oil. The car would be filled at Ponca City, Oklahoma, and be sent to Kansas City's Argentine Yard to await the arrival of the locomotive. If the 103 didn't bring it along, fuel would be hard to come by out on the railroad. The tank car usually would be placed in the train just behind the dynamometer and business cars.

H. B. Lautz, the Eastern Lines' general manager, wrote his superintendents on December 22, 1939, that the plan was to handle 3,500 tons from Chicago's Corwith Yard to Wellington, the western extremity of the Eastern Lines, in no more than 100 cars. Another letter advised that the 103 would run through to San Bernardino on an 86-hour schedule out of Chicago. If there weren't 3,500 tons for the West at Emporia, the yard was instructed to fill out the train with empty refrigerator cars for Wellington. Westbound on the eastern end of the railroad, the 103 would be fueled and watered at Argentine and Wellington. Eastbound, with like tonnage, it would take fuel and water at Clovis, New Mexico, and Argentine.

On December 28, Purcell put out a long letter. He reported that half the 103 would be delivered to the Santa Fe at Corwith that same day. It would undergo tests of its automatic train control equipment, which wasn't altogether compatible with the system the Santa Fe had in service around East Fort Madison on the Illinois Division. The train control would permit a maximum speed of 55 miles an hour, the speed limit for steam-powered freight trains.

Purcell noted that the 103 had a speed-control governor that in non-train-control territory would let it run as fast as 73 miles per hour, but no faster. He promulgated lengthy instructions for enginemen on the train control and on how to handle the throttle.

The test train would highball out of Corwith as soon as No. 11, the westbound *Kansas Cityan*, was by. Air-brake inspections en route were to be expedited. Roller bearings being almost unheard of on freight cars in those days, journal boxes on all cars in the train were to be serviced and oiled at Corwith and all regular oiling stations. The 103 was to be uncoupled from its train only for watering and fueling, for which it would set out the tank car on an adjacent track.

Where crews changed but the locomotive need not be uncoupled, the new crew was to be driven to the train. This arrangement

THE BEST OF BOTH RAIL WORLDS
By John Shedd Reed

John Shedd Reed. Trains *magazine, Kalmbach Media*

Editor's note: John Shedd Reed was president, Atchison, Topeka and Santa Fe Railway, 1967–1978.

I was a steam locomotive devotee whose ambition to become an engineer had been frustrated by the Depression of the 1930s. I was grateful to land a job in the locomotive testing department of the Santa Fe upon graduating from Yale in 1939. The many hundreds of miles I then spent riding the Santa Fe's most modern steam engine were most gratifying. I doubt there is a more exciting experience than riding atop the cylinder at the front of a giant 4-8-4 traveling 90 miles per hour, taking readings and keeping a nervous watch on the rails ahead, hoping a truck had not stalled on a crossing.

Little did I anticipate that this environment would suddenly be changed by an intruder, the first diesel-electric locomotive designed specifically for freight service. When my Test Department was given the task of evaluating the performance of Electro-Motive Corporation's experimental 103 and subsequently the Santa Fe's own 100, it became my bittersweet lot to witness at first hand a revolution in railway motive power.

On the transcontinental tests of engine 103, my primary job was to operate the chronograph in the dynamometer car coupled behind the locomotive, although members of the test crew frequently rotated assignments, which included making observations in the engine room and the cab.

Those early test runs were not without a few moments of glory for this would-be engineer. While most of the actual operation of the engine was personally handled by our system air-brake supervisor, he had to be given a few hours of rest during the long trip. I occasionally found myself in the cab with an engineer who had never set foot on a diesel. He was understandably lost as he sat at the new controls.

"Hey kid, how do you run this thing?"

It fell to me to coach him on how to start the train: by pulling out the controller handle slowly rather than by jerking it out rapidly, as he would the throttle on a steam engine. We had an absolute prohibition on the use of sand, normally used to increase the adhesion of wheel to rail. So, here was the young Test Department assistant, instructing veterans in methods they found difficult to accept!

As the test runs progressed, the feeling of impending change was persuasive. I recall many small crew-change towns where crowds of railway employees and their families had come down to watch the interloper pass through. Their glum faces revealed their realization that this new diesel was handling twice the tonnage of the prevailing 3800-class steam engines. They were obviously making mental calculations as to the diesel's impact on future employment.

I could not help thinking of the Luddites in early 19th-century England as they rioted against new labor-saving textile machinery. Fortunately, the railways escaped that kind of violence, yet they faced decades of resistance from the industry's labor unions.

Dieselization of the Santa Fe led in turn to a redesign of a railroad itself—extensive physical changes and a modification of the operating philosophy of the system. In steam days, each operating division had its own assignment of engines and there was a degree of competition and sometimes noncooperation between adjoining divisions. Extending locomotive runs across the country, already begun with modern steam engines, led to a spirit of cooperation.

As one who had been enamored of the old way of running a railroad but who had been trained to be "always on the move toward a better way," I am glad that I saw the best of both worlds. I had seen steam power at its very best; I played a small part in the diesel revolution so critical to America's railways.

The crew of the 103's demonstration trip poses with the diesels at Keenbrook, California, at the southern approach of Cajon Pass, January 17, 1940. *Photo John Angold Collection, Wallace W. Abbey Collection*

Three officials, likely of the Santa Fe, occupy the cupola of the dynamometer car during tests of the 103. The man on the right is keeping track of passing mileposts. *Photo Santa Fe Railway, Trains magazine, Kalmbach Media*

brought no protests, apparently, from the unions, even though labor agreements required crew exchanges at the roundhouse.

A road foreman of engines and an assistant air-brake supervisor were to be aboard the 103 at all times, Purcell instructed. Pool and chain-gang locomotive engineers and firemen would be assigned. The total population in the cab was never to be more than five.

Two business cars, the 3 and the 31, would be on the rear of the train. Purcell warned that heating plants or Baker heaters on these and any other business cars that joined the test should be in good working order. It was winter, and it was going to get cold.

Purcell's instructions on how to handle the controls of the 103 doubtless had come from Electro-Motive. They were far different from any instructions on how to handle the levers and valves of a steam locomotive. In due course, they'd be honored in the breach many times, at a cost of broken knuckles, parted trains, and badly kicked-about lading. No one had ever before seen a locomotive that developed its maximum pulling power at low speeds rather than at high speeds. Dilworth observed later that the 103 pulled many trains in two.

Few who would be called upon to operate the 103 had ever been aboard a diesel. Jobs on what few passenger diesels were in service usually went to the engineers and firemen with the most seniority. It was likely the 103 would draw newer crew members, perhaps even men off the extra board.

In starting, the engineer needed to "make sure and be positive" the brakes were released throughout the train, allowing 3.5 to 5 minutes. He should check all gauges. Then he should open the throttle only to the first of the eight notches and leave it there until the train was stretched—until all the slack was out of it. Only then should he widen on the throttle, leaving it in each notch six or seven seconds so the locomotive could absorb the change in load. When the wheel-slip light flashed, indicating the electrical connections to the traction motors had gone from series to parallel, he should close the throttle to the notch that would hold the train's speed where he wanted it to be, always allowing three or four seconds in each notch.

In an emergency, however, the engineer should feel free to close the throttle all the way without hesitation. But, Purcell's instructions warned, "Emergency does not include oversight on the part of engineer failing to watch train speed and poor judgment of distance."

By December 29, the plan was for the first test run to begin at Corwith either the night of January 2 or the morning of January 3, 1940. There'd been talk of deadheading the 103 from Argentine up to Topeka so it could be weighed at the shop there, but now that wasn't going to happen. The 103 would go straight through to San Bernardino. It would be weighed at Topeka on the way back.

By December 30, the plan was that the 103 would power No. 43, the *Northern California Fast Freight*, out of Corwith at 9:30 a.m. on January 3, as No. 11 was departing Dearborn Station. The schedule allowed 12 hours to get the train over the 450 miles to Argentine. Once there, the locomotive, the dynamometer car, the fuel car, and business car 3 would be run up to Topeka, where the locomotive would be fueled, watered, and weighed. The 103 would come back to Argentine the night of January 4 and would leave the morning of January 5 for San Bernardino.

The crew of that matchbox on wheels, dynamometer car 29, was going to have a busy time. Twenty-two tests were ahead; westbound, the tests were odd numbers, eastbound, even.

On each test run the crew would record the 103's speed and effort in millions of foot-pounds at the drawbar. Members of the test crew in the 29's cupola would log starts and stops; they would time to the second passing stations and mileposts. Observers in the 103's cab would keep a continuous record of throttle positions and the manner in which the traction motors were connected electrically. Observers in the engine rooms would note the revolutions per minute of the diesel prime movers, temperature of the cooling water, and fuel and lube-oil pressures. They'd watch out for anything unusual.

At 30 seconds past 10:24 a.m. on January 3, 1940, almost an hour late, the 103 snaked its train, 43's extra, around the wye and out of Corwith on test No. 1. In the 99-car, 3,345-ton consist were 33 loads and 66 empties.

Except for a drawbar that broke on the 41st car as the train started up from the mandatory stop at the New York Central crossing at Streator, run No. 1 was uneventful. The 103 muscled its train from Chillicothe up the 1.1 percent grade of Edelstein Hill at 16 miles an hour without the usual helper. After pausing to let a group of visitors off at Main Street in Kansas City, 43 stopped in Argentine Yard at 12:12 a.m. The 103 was taken to Topeka to stand on the scale.

There was concern that 3,500 tons wouldn't be available for California at Argentine on January 5. Argentine was instructed to hold sufficient California traffic on January 3 and 4, not to include freight-forwarder traffic that had been earmarked for an earlier 43. Out of Argentine the 103's train would consist of a block of 2,150 tons of the "oldest" California traffic, which the 103 would move all the way to San Bernardino. The remainder of the tonnage would be cut off at Gallup so the train wouldn't violate Arizona's 70-car limit.

By January 4, train dispatchers west of Argentine were advised to "give connecting divisions close call figures as enginemen are to be on hand to change crews without delay."

Fred Gurley's car, the 34, was coming out to Argentine from Chicago on No. 7, the *Fast Mail Express*. It would be on the rear of the test train with the 32 and the 31. On the morning of January 5, car 37 would be brought down from Topeka on No. 128, the local passenger train. It would be in the test train as far as Wellington, presumably with the Eastern Lines' general manager aboard.

Late on the afternoon of January 4, with the test train already well out of Corwith, new instructions were put out about Purcell's car, the 31: Don't take it off No. 1, the *Scout*, at Kansas City so a switch engine could take it to Argentine. Instead, put it on No. 27, the *Antelope*, for Topeka.

By the morning of January 5, just before its departure from Argentine, the test train's consist looked like this: the 103; dynamometer car 29; business car 32; the tank car of diesel fuel; the revenue business consisting of 79 loads and 1 empty "RD"—Santa Fe Refrigerator Department—car; and business cars 34 and 37. Running as No. 43's extra, the 103 and its cars got out at 11:19 a.m. The train's weight: 3,674 tons. That's what the Operating Department figured. In the Test Department's dynamometer car, the train weighed 3,660 tons.

Forty-three was into Emporia at 2:14 p.m. and out at 2:29. There was a slight delay at Merrick at the west end of Emporia's yard. The conductor dropped off a penciled message that, down the road, would be relayed to Superintendent Claude Cravens in the business car on the head end: "My register out of Emporia should read 77 special, 1 dead freight, 1 empty refrigerator, 1 empty tank, 1 dynamometer, 1 caboose, 3,689 tons. The delay at Merrick was on account of brakes sticking on biz car, fixed Emporia. Seem to be running cool, train so far in good shape."

The second test, run 3, from Argentine to San Bernardino between January 5 and 8, didn't go as well as had run 1 out of Corwith. The trouble had more to do with the train than with the locomotive. Some of the troubles might have come from how the train was being handled with the new locomotive, but the test report only hinted at that.

Minimum speeds up some of the grades on the eastern end of the run were comfortably in the 20s and 30s. But out of Waynoka, Oklahoma, the fuel line to the engine in the B section of the trailing locomotive froze. With a fourth of its power gone, the 103 was able to manage only 14 miles an hour up the 1.0 percent grade of Curtis Hill. But it managed.

Almost 300 tons were added to the train at Clovis, effectively cutting a little off its speed on the hills west of there. Fueling and watering the 103—once again a 5,400-horsepower machine—plus changing the train's crew cost 1 hour, 19 minutes of dead time.

Later, passing the town of Mountainair and starting down through Abo Canyon toward Belen and the Rio Grande, a knuckle broke on business car 32. There went 42 minutes at Belen while the knuckle was replaced.

Forty-three came out of Belen with 3,636 tons in 91 cars. It climbed the 1.25 percent grade up to Dalies in 40 minutes at no slower than 15 miles an hour. It stopped in the yard at Gallup at 2:21 a.m., where it was reduced to meet Arizona's train-length law. An hour later it was on its way again. But in Arizona, between Adamana and Holbrook, a drawbar pulled out of a tank car. The car was set out. With the train stitched together again and the 103 pulling, the front coupler on the tank car of diesel fuel broke. The car was placed ahead of the locomotive—how, the test report doesn't tell us—and the 103 shoved it to Winslow.

The Holbrook incident cost 2 hours, 8 minutes. Servicing the 103 at Winslow and applying a new coupler to the tank car cost 1 hour, 41 minutes of terminal delay.

Ahead now was the climb up to the Arizona Divide and the descent to Seligman, 142 miles of unforgiving railroad. The 103 was going to try it without a helper. At Winslow its train had been reduced to 2,400 tons in 58 cars. It was snowing and the rail over toward Seligman was wet. The thermometer was hovering around the freezing mark.

Climbing the 62.3-mile, 1.42 percent grade from Winslow to Riordan, the 103 never dropped below 18 miles an hour. The train stopped at Supai for an air test and so the retainers could be turned up to hold some air in the brake cylinders on the trip back

The builder's plate of the original 103, as it appears today on the lead unit at the National Museum of Transport in St. Louis. *Photo Wallace W. Abbey, Center for Railroad Photography & Art Collection*

down the hill. At Daze, the train stopped for an inspection and to let the wheels cool, and it stopped again at milepost 400.4 so the retainers could be turned back down. It was at Seligman a few seconds shy of 5:01 p.m. The 103 had come over the Arizona Divide and the other grades on the Third District of the Albuquerque Division in 5 hours, 56 minutes, of which 5 hours, 17 minutes constituted its actual running time.

Forty-three was underway again out of Seligman at 4:21 p.m., now on Pacific standard time. Through Needles and Barstow to San Bernardino, it went right along with no unusual circumstances, except that west of Pisgah the train ran off and left its conductor. Six minutes later he was back aboard the way car.

Just beyond Barstow, the test train went into a siding to let the eastbound *Super Chief* by. Then the 103 dug in for the pull over

American Society of Mechanical Engineers plaque on the 103 at the Museum of Transport attests to the 103's landmark status. *Photo Wallace W. Abbey, Center for Railroad Photography & Art Collection*

Cajon Pass. It stopped at Summit at 7:24 a.m. for an air test and to set up retainers, a five-minute process. Coming down the hill, it stopped at Cajon and again at Devore to cool the wheels and for inspection. The retainers were turned back down at Highland Junction. At 9:29 a.m., the 103 and its charges arrived at San Bernardino. Test No. 3 was history.

The 103 needed a doctor. Electro-Motive representatives who were accompanying the test inspected it thoroughly, inside and out. The main generators and traction motors were cleaned; the latter's suspension bearings were lubricated. Special attention was paid to the porcelain insulators. New piping was installed so the Purolator fuel filters could be bypassed should they plug up. The engine that had failed got a new governor. The test report didn't say where such replacement parts were coming from, but it's likely a boxcar of parts and tools was not far back in the train.

Eight wheels under the locomotive exhibited thermal cracks or flat spots. One pair was put on a wheel lathe and reduced in diameter by better than 2 inches from its original 38.5.

Test 4 began at San Bernardino on January 9, at the pointy end of the first *Green Fruit Express* of the day. The 103 took 1 hour, 38 minutes to go from "Berdoo" up to Summit with its train of 1,759 tons in 37 cars, without a helper. Once beyond Cajon Pass at Barstow, the train was filled to 3,420 tons in 62 cars. The GFX and its green-and-gold locomotive arrived at Winslow at 8:54 a.m. on January 10. The 103 hadn't needed help on the ruling grade from Ash Fork up to Supai.

Run 5 took the test train from Winslow back to Barstow on January 10 and 11. The 103 waltzed up the 1.42 percent grade to the Arizona Divide at Riordan with the 54 cars and 2,098 tons of an extra at no slower than 19 miles an hour. An hour and a half after it arrived at Barstow, it was headed north for Bakersfield on test 5A. By 11:39 a.m. it was there, having brought 1,738 tons over Tehachapi Pass at a minimum speed of 14 miles an hour, without a helper.

Soon the 103 was headed back south with a VMX train on test No. 6. It didn't need help over Tehachapi in this direction, either. An hour after its arrival at Barstow, the 103 was starting run 7, heading back for San Bernardino with the VMX. It was still January 11. Not even the most modern steam locomotive could have equaled that utilization.

Factory representatives were at San Bernardino again to check out the 103, so it was held out of service until the morning of January 13. Everything on it that could be checked, inspected, cleaned, adjusted, drained, refilled, repacked, lubricated, or otherwise tended to received attention. Two power assemblies in one engine received new cylinder heads. One of the steam generators got a new water pump. The contact fingers in the load regulators in all units were checked and some were replaced. One of the air compressors needed its valves repaired. Several wheels displayed cracks across their treads, but the test report doesn't say whether the wheels were changed out.

Run 8: At 6:56 a.m. on January 13, without a helper over Cajon, the 103 lifted 2,011 tons in the 41 cars of a CTX out of San Bernardino and headed for Winslow. It was in Barstow at 10:15 a.m., where its train was filled out. The 103 got out of Barstow at 11:27 a.m. with 80 cars, 3,815 tons.

The locomotive was serviced at Needles while the train was reduced to 2,891 tons in 64 cars. That took an hour and a half. Out of Needles at 7:33 p.m., the 103 required 4 hours, 56 minutes to climb up to Yampai, 122.5 miles, always moving at least 18 miles an hour. It arrived at Seligman at 1:39 a.m. and departed at 3:17 a.m., now on mountain standard time.

The test report doesn't track well the officials, other experts, and guests in the business cars on the test runs, although indications are that there were quite a few of them. It does report, however, that on this run cars 38, 39, and 40 came out of the train at Ash Fork.

Again, no helper was necessary from Ash Fork up to Supai. On the downhill run from Riordan, the train stopped for 11 minutes at Angell to let the wheels cool. It was into Winslow at 9:43 p.m. The weather had been clear, the temperature a bit below freezing, the wind mild, the rail frosty to dry.

On January 14 and 15, the 103 pedaled from Winslow over to Barstow on test run 9 with the third section of a 43 train. But first the 103 had to stand at Winslow for 2 hours, 42 minutes waiting for Third 43 to show up. The trip was uneventful, except that the train orders weren't ready at Cadiz, California, creating a five-minute delay. More significant was the 26-minute delay at Homer waiting for the *El Capitan* to go by and the 32-minute delay at Bagdad waiting for the *Super Chief*. It was 6:52 a.m. on January 15 when Third 43 arrived at Barstow.

One hour six minutes later, with a combination of three trains—43, Third 43, and an NCX—the 103 highballed for Bakersfield with test 9A. The 53 cars weighed 2,179 tons. The run was so routine that the discussion about it consumed only six lines in the test report. Explaining what had occurred on some of the other tests took many paragraphs.

Coming back to Barstow later the same day on test 10 with an even lighter VMX, the 103 did fine, but its running time of 5 hours, 9 minutes was spoiled by 57 minutes of dead time on the road. The test train spent a lot of time waiting in sidings for other trains. It didn't get to Barstow until 7:50 p.m.

Test 11 left Barstow for San Bernardino on January 15, 49 minutes after the equipment had completed test 10. Again, the run was routine, seven lines in the report. And again, on its arrival at San Bernardino, the 103 was poked, prodded, and otherwise prepped for test 12, a trip back to Clovis that would begin the morning of January 17.

Other than pausing at Needles for 2.5 hours so the brake shoes could be changed on the dynamometer car and on business car 32, the only out-of-the-ordinary event on test 12 was a delay of 2 hours, 19 minutes at Keenbrook for the company photographer.

The 103 then did two round trips between Clovis and Belen on January 20, 21, and 22. On test run 13, its 33 train broke in two when a knuckle opened five cars from the rear of the train. After run 16, the 103 underwent routine checking and maintenance at Clovis.

The means of communication would be called archaic today, but the wires and traingrams that chronicled these tests said some interesting things about railroading on the Santa Fe in early 1940 and about Electro-Motive's experimental 103 and its use.

As the 103 returned to Chicago from Clovis on January 23, officials on the Eastern Division received this wire: "Third GFXT-14 with diesel engine 103 now reaching Wellington 5:50 p.m. and will run around PGXT at Wellington. The way they are moving on the Panhandle Division should reach Emporia about 9:30 p.m. Train consists of 114 redballs including 1 oranges St. Joe and 1 lemons Concordia 3 dead freight business cars 406 and 32 and 3 baggage cars 6,033 tons." The 103, with its Third GFX, actually arrived at Emporia more than two hours behind that figure.

That same morning, Cravens, aboard the test train, got this wire at Newton: "Would appreciate you having your supts biz car at Wellington to go into diesel test train and go as far as Shopton for purpose of providing sleeping quarters for test crew and for serving meals to 12 men."

The reply from Cravens reached the Extra EMC 103 East at Waynoka: "Am arranging put business car 406 in diesel train Wellington this p.m. to go through to Shopton with supplies for 50 meals." He would send the car from Newton west to Wellington in No. 1, the *Scout*, later that day. As it happened, car 406 would stay with the test train all the way to Chicago. It would come back on the next westbound run.

This wire moved to Newton from Topeka shortly after noon on January 26: "Expect run test train with diesel locomotive 103 out of Corwith approximately 9 a.m. tomorrow 27th to run through to Clovis. Should have 2,500 tons out Corwith consisting of loads. Expect arrive Emporia about 6 a.m. 28th where should pick up seven boxcars with map and slogan arriving Wellington about 11 a.m. same date where refrig cars from Wichita with map and slogan will be placed in train for taking photographs. These should move Wichita to Wellington not later than [train] 69 tomorrow night."

A later wire indicated that West Wichita Shops would release four refrigerator cars "with new type stenciling" later that day. The Santa Fe would become modestly famous for the simplified map of its routes it applied to the sides of its box and refrigerator cars. According to some of the popular railroad press, hoboes and other itinerants appreciated the service.

The seven boxcars, rebuilds, were waiting at Emporia when the test train got there. It took just 12 minutes to double them into the train.

On January 27, a wire from Chicago had reported that the day's 2,500-ton test train needed to be moved right along so it would be at Wellington under "suitable conditions for photographs." The run was the last westbound test with the entire locomotive. The photo shoot took place 12 telegraph poles east of Southern Kansas Junction, which was just east of Wellington, and consumed 1 hour and 21 minutes. The dispatcher had been instructed to protect the train with a train order.

A 6,010-ton third GFX, eastbound behind the 103, dragged out of Clovis before dawn on January 23, taking 20 minutes to go the first two miles while the rear brakeman lined back the switches. After that, it was highball all the way to Argentine with run No. 18. (There inexplicably had been no run 17.) Except at crew-change points, the train didn't stop. It arrived at Argentine Yard at 3:17 a.m. on January 24.

EMC's 103 leads Santa Fe train 4 through a curve at Nelson, Arizona, during the January 1940 eastbound demonstration trip.
Photo D. L. Ingersoll, Wallace W. Abbey Collection

Most of the cars in its train had Kansas City as their destination, so the 103 was held for 10.5 hours while a new train was built for it. During this delay it was serviced, and a single cylinder head was changed; a gasket had been leaking and the cylinder was filling with water. With a 4,818-ton 42 train of 94 cars, test 18 resumed at Argentine at 1:51 p.m. on January 24.

It was now very cold. The temperature at Argentine had been just a few degrees above zero, the wind 28 miles an hour. Over on the Missouri Division, the wind was even stronger, the temperature as low as minus 8. The wind was stronger still east of Shopton, where the temperature sank to minus 13. Brakes in the train frequently were sticking and wheels were being flattened. In the engine rooms of the 103, the test crew was fearful the diesels wouldn't stay warm enough to work properly.

At Corwith, the 103 underwent a thorough examination, some repair, and a temporary modification: the drive shafts to the cooling fans at one end of each section were removed so some of the warm air from the radiators would stay in the engine rooms.

Weather conditions hadn't improved much as the 103 started back to Clovis on January 27 with No. 43, on test 19. Four times between Corwith and Chillicothe the train was delayed by a frozen train line or by brake defects. The 103 was serviced again on its arrival at Clovis. This time, the list of things to do to it was considerably shorter.

Run 20, from Clovis back to Corwith, was like the Santa Fe wanted them all to be. The temperature was above freezing and sometimes well into the 50s, although it dropped gradually as the train came east. Twice the test GFX had to stop so a hot journal bearing could be doctored. The test train lost 14 minutes at Marceline, Missouri, waiting for No. 24, the *Grand Canyon Limited*, to finish its station work. It lost a few minutes more coming into Surrey because No. 12, the *Chicagoan*, was ahead of it.

The test report doesn't tell us why the rear section of the 103, serial number 103O, was uncoupled at Corwith on January 31 and delivered back to La Grange. Perhaps the Santa Fe wanted to run tests with just 2,700 horsepower. Maybe a trip back to the factory was in order for half the locomotive.

The remaining half of the 103 made another round trip to Clovis. It got out of Corwith at 10:31 a.m. the same day, towing the 2,069 tons of First 43 in 50 loads and 2 empties. With no more tonnage than that it went right along. It started back for Corwith from Clovis at 7:05 a.m. on February 2 with the 3,528 tons of the third GFX. Other than several delays in meeting westbound trains on the single-track Southern District, the trip could have been called average. But when it stopped to let the *Chicagoan* by at Ethel, the brakes on the rear truck of the A section didn't release. All four wheels were flattened.

This second half of the 103 was released to Electro-Motive upon its arrival at Corwith. With it went a moderate list of work to be done; except for replacing the flat wheels, none was major.

That alone was a singular accomplishment, given the thousands of miles and tens of thousands of tons under the 103's belt. But there would be very little rest. By the middle of the month, the locomotive would be off again to complete all 83,000 miles of its testing.

Santa Fe's ultimate steam locomotive, 2-10-4 No. 5032, rolls off the turntable at Clovis, New Mexico, ready to take a freight east over the Plains Division in 1952. *Photo Stan Kistler*

EIGHT LESSONS LEARNED FROM THE 103

What the 103 Did, and Did Not Do, on the Santa Fe

IN THE 32 DAYS DURING WHICH EMC'S 103 WAS TESTED ON the Santa Fe, it covered 12,312 miles in road service. It was on the road 512 hours and 2 minutes. Of this, 390 hours, 3 minutes were spent pulling trains. The balance was delay time on the road or at intermediate terminals. Its utilization—time on the road against total time in service—was 67.3 percent, according to the test report published May 13, 1940.

Fuel lines had frozen once, and a defective governor required the speed of one engine to be controlled by hand at one point. Otherwise, all four prime movers functioned well.

According to the report's summary, the automatic transition hadn't been altogether satisfactory. Transition from series to parallel and parallel to shunt occurred automatically at prescribed speeds and throttle positions, as did transition from shunt back to parallel. But transition from parallel back to series required that the throttle be closed.

This manual step didn't cause much of a problem; Electro-Motive's onboard representative would quickly open and close the main control switch. This put the locomotive through the downward transition without loss of speed, one of those little tricks that wasn't mentioned in the manual. But the test report recommended "some automatic or cab-controlled method for shifting from parallel to series operation."

The report noted, however, that "continuous operation in series at speeds from 14 to 20 miles per hour for periods of over two hours indicated that the engines and motors functioned without overheating."

Consensus was that the 5,400-horsepower 103 was definitely superior to a 5001-class 2-10-4 steam locomotive at speeds up to 29 miles an hour. At faster speeds, the diesel's power was only slightly less than a 5001's. Moreover, a 2,700-horsepower Model F was superior to a 4101-class 2-8-4 across the entire range of freight train speeds. Over nearly all districts, the 103 and its train equaled or bettered the fastest freight train schedules.

Ample capacity to cool the engines was always available, the report said, and "where temperatures have approached the maximum, it is the result of the attendant being otherwise occupied and not giving the ventilator adjustment prompt attention."

On some runs in mountain territory, the air brakes had been used as much as 70 percent of the time. "Consideration should be given to application of partial regenerative braking to control speeds, with application of conventional brakes to wheels only in cases of stopping or auxiliary control," the report recommended.

By eliminating stops to cool wheels, regenerative (dynamic) braking would save as much as three hours between Winslow and San Bernardino. Not only that, but a number of wheels had been damaged by heavy air-braking. That wouldn't have

Facing, The crew of 103's first trip would have had this view of the east tunnel portal at Johnson Canyon in Arizona, since abandoned by Santa Fe in a realignment. *Photo Jack Delano, Prints & Photographs Division, Library of Congress*

RAPID PROGRESS OF RAILROADS

Editor's note: The following is a news story about the test of the 103, taken from the January 25, 1940, edition of the Winslow (Arizona) Mail.

"Development of railroads during the last three years has been more rapid than at any other time since their construction in pioneer days," said E. J. Engel, president of the AT&SF Railway, who concluded a two-day inspection trip here last week. He passed through Winslow the first part of the week. Engel, who has headquarters in Chicago, was accompanied by W. K. Etter, vice president, Chicago; E. E. McCarty, general manager, Los Angeles; F. J. MacKie, assistant manager, Los Angeles; and a group of Arizonans.

"During the last three years I believe the railroads have developed more than any other form of transportation including the airways, waterways, and highways," said Engel. "Development of light streamlined equipment with diesel power is bringing about swift changes with which the railroads are keeping pace."

Before his departure for Chicago, Engel disclosed that the Santa Fe, not content with using diesel-powered locomotives for pulling passenger trains, is now experimenting with them for hauling freight. A different type of locomotive is being developed for pulling these trains, Engel said. Tests are being made between Winslow and San Bernardino and between Barstow and Bakersfield, California.

Power is applied directly to the driving wheels in the new locomotives. The engines are of 5,400 horsepower. Tests in northern Arizona began [early in January], soon after the new diesels were delivered, according to Engel.

"Performance so far has been quite satisfactory," Engel said, "but we do not want to get out on a limb by talking too much about it yet."

---

happened had the 103 had dynamic brakes. Electro-Motive was well aware of such brake technology in Europe, but at the time of the tests there was no such thing for the Model F. Dynamic brakes would be included in later tests.

Little information remains about how the many guests from other railroads and elsewhere who rode along on the tests of the 103 had reacted to what they experienced. One report, that of Lewis D. Freeman, exists. It was preserved thanks to legendary deep thinker and academic packrat John W. Barriger III, who after the war served as president for several railroads, including the Monon and Pittsburgh & Lake Erie. At the time of the 103 tests, Barriger was head of the Reconstruction Finance Corporation (RFC), a federal agency created at the end of the Hoover administration.

Lewis Freeman, an examiner for the Railroad Division of the RFC, came east behind the 103 from Amarillo to Corwith on January 23, 1940. Later, he would ride a westbound Northern Pacific test between Laurel and Auburn.

Freeman reported that the 103 developed a very high drawbar pull, approximately half the ultimate strength of the current AAR standard freight-car couplers. He said, "It is reasonably certain this 5,400-horsepower unit represents the maximum size that can be built with existing freight cars."

Between Kansas City and Chicago, freezing water in the air-brake system of freight cars interfered with braking operation

Chronograph operator in the dynamometer car records the performance of the 100's first exhibition trip west in March 1941. *Photo Santa Fe Railway,* Trains *magazine, Kalmbach Media*

Above and facing, Lewis D. Freeman of the Reconstruction Finance Corporation rode the test run of EMC 103 and photographed the diesels and their train during a stop at Canadian, Texas, in January 1940. *Photos Lewis D. Freeman, Barriger National Railroad Library, St. Louis Mercantile Library at University of Missouri-St. Louis*

and caused delays. Freeman noted: "In spite of this difficulty, the locomotive performance was excellent and in many respects superior to steam locomotive performance under similar conditions."

Freeman added that the fixed-drawbar connections between the two sections of each unit made it inadvisable to use the 103 in pusher service. "This feature can be corrected in future designs," Freeman wrote. Indeed, Santa Fe's two-unit Model Fs would have standard couplers, not the links associated with the A and B sections of the 103.

He had this to say about crew size: "In addition to the locomotive engineman and fireman required by agreement with train-service organizations, there will be at least one and possibly two maintainers required to ride on the diesel locomotive to attend to the engines, lubricate them, and make such repairs and adjustments as are necessary."

Freeman noted what others had also observed: All the weight of the diesel was utilized as "adhesive" weight, whereas only about 32 percent of the total weight of a modern 4-8-4 and its tender would directly transfer power to the rail.

What bottom-line conclusions did Lewis Freeman draw about the economic value of the diesel? He hedged somewhat in his government-speak, indicating that the economic justification remained to be demonstrated: "The high initial cost of these modern diesel-electric locomotives and the unknown ultimate life combined with the more intensive utilization demanded by the high first cost seems to indicate that the period of amortization should be set at not more than 10 years, as compared with the usual 15-year period for steam locomotives."

In contrast, the Santa Fe's own Test Department was more definitive. It gave the Model F high marks: "The performance of locomotive 103 during tests was highly creditable. The two-unit [5,400-horsepower] locomotive showed a hauling capacity superior to that of the heaviest steam freight locomotives. Excepting for unusual delays, heavier trains were handled in running time equal to or superior to that of expedited trains. The use of the single-unit [2,700-horsepower] locomotive on the lighter trains demonstrated the flexibility of having multiple-unit power."

The 103 had handled nearly all test trains without helpers and demonstrated the capability to do without them hauling maximum tonnage over all distances. Exceptions were San Bernardino to Summit, Mojave to Eric, Bakersfield to Summit

Switch, Ash Fork to Supai, and Belen to Mountainair, over the freight line by way of the Southern District.

The Test Department concluded: "The test of this type of diesel locomotive has proven its worth as a high-speed freight locomotive, and it is recommended that sufficient number be secured to thoroughly determine its serviceability and economy."

That said, the Test Department thought the Model F could be improved. It made 26 specific recommendations, including increasing the air supply to the steam generators, eliminating vibrations from the diesel engines and air compressors, and adding a water glass to the cooling system so the tanks would not be overfilled and thus subject to freezing.

There were several other problems to address:

- Control of the temperature of cooling water needed to be improved. Clutches in the fan drives would allow any or all fans to be shut off so warm air from the radiators could remain in the engine rooms.
- Exhaust gases coming out of the stacks tended to be sucked back into the engine rooms.
- The reverser didn't have a "neutral" position, so someone had to ride along in the cab to reposition the reverser lever as the locomotive was being shunted back and forth in the yard.
- The main generator needed to be more robust and required a redesign.
- Fully automatic transition was necessary to eliminate the possibility of operator error. Transition should be timed so all sections didn't "shift" at the same moment, which jerked the train unacceptably.
- Ventilators should be provided in the roof to eliminate a partial vacuum in the engine rooms. Baffles placed below the air-intake filters would prevent cold air from blowing down on employees and would also keep water out.
- AAR couplers with heavy safety chains between sections were desirable instead of drawbars. Each power plant should be made self-sustaining by providing a separate battery for each section.
- Control circuits and air-brake piping should be arranged to conform to present passenger diesel locomotive units. If so arranged, the only change required to permit use in passenger service would be in the gear ratio.

Another recommendation seemed to suggest the FTs might show up in passenger service. The report pushed for larger wheels on "freight versions": 50 inches or more in diameter, up from 38 inches. The larger wheels would only raise the center of gravity six inches but would also improve mileage between wheel-turnings and reduce stress on the rails, especially if dynamic braking was not provided.

Several of the recommendations became the basis for modifications to the production locomotives that would soon go to the Santa Fe and other roads.

As it was and given where it had been and what it had done—performed like a combination of a Mikado, Santa Fe, and Mallet—the 103 was persuasive, if persuasion was still necessary. Even before the 103 got back to La Grange in October 1940 after its full regimen of tests across the country, the Santa Fe handed Electro-Motive an order for two production copies.

Facing, During its western exhibition trip in 1940, the 103 pauses beneath the 27th Street bridge at the Milwaukee Road's West Milwaukee terminal. Trains *magazine, Kalmbach Media*

NINE A BIG COMING-OUT PARTY

Santa Fe Rolls Out Its First Freight Diesel

SOMETIMES, THE MINUTES OF MEETINGS OF CORPORATE boards of directors are fascinating for what they tell us. Sometimes, they're frustrating because they do no more than hint. For example, the minutes of the meeting of Santa Fe's board on June 25, 1940, report that this item came up: "The President [Edward J. Engel] referred to the need for increased motive power for handling of the company's business and recommended that authority be granted to acquire 10 additional steam passenger locomotives at a cost of approximately $2 million and two 5,400-horsepower diesel freight locomotives at a cost of approximately $1 million." The board approved the expenditures. Evidently, the locomotives would be bought with cash.

What the minutes don't tell us is what Santa Fe intended to do with those diesels; what studies had been made to justify the million-dollar appropriation, which wasn't in the budget; and who made the studies. Nor do the minutes say who justified to the board why the fundamental nature of Santa Fe's freight locomotives should change, especially when a new batch of steam locomotives, which would become 4-8-4s Nos. 3776–3785, was part of the same authorization.

Given Santa Fe's long allegiance to steam power, a fly on the wall might have heard an interesting discussion, indeed.

Certainly, the tests of Electro-Motive's experimental 103 on the Santa Fe the previous winter were a major factor. One might conclude, based on the potential economic return on commercial copies of the 103, the diesels would be a shoo-in. But for all its progressiveness, the Santa Fe could be a careful, conservative railroad. It wasn't known to make snap decisions. Especially big ones.

No doubt, Fred Gurley had a lot to do with the proposal. Gurley may have been the industry's leading proponent of, and executive expert on, diesel-electric locomotives. The Santa Fe's board had enticed him away from the Burlington in 1939 with a near-the-top, vice-presidential job and the understanding he would be Santa Fe's next president.

Since his Burlington days, Gurley had advocated diesel-electrics, first as switchers and then for passenger service. He'd written and spoken publicly about the advantages of diesels, at times a lone voice in a steam-oriented world. He had organized the nonstop run of the Burlington's diesel-powered *Pioneer Zephyr* from Denver to Chicago in 1934.

Santa Fe's board had sought him out because it was uncomfortable with the line of succession to the presidency once Engel would retire, and Engel's health wasn't the best. It's also likely directors were impressed with Gurley's view of motive power.

Moreover, the Santa Fe recently had been looking at the idea of speeding up its transcontinental freight trains. It had studied the feasibility of 92-hour schedules for its California–Chicago *Green Fruit Express* that would lop off many hours.

Facing, An FT car body, quite possibly the first one built as demonstrator 103, is lowered onto its trucks at the EMC factory. *Photo Santa Fe Railway,* Trains *magazine, Kalmbach Media*

Santa Fe's new FT diesel-electric flanked by steam locomotives at Fort Madison, Iowa, December 1940. *Photo Santa Fe Railway, Wallace W. Abbey Collection*

Certainly, a service like that would be far easier to provide with diesels than with even the best and newest steam locomotives.

It could be assumed that diesels for freight service had been a hot topic in the Mechanical, Operating, and Executive Departments of the Santa Fe even before EMC announced it was coming up with a freight locomotive. Electro-Motive certainly would have sought the views of a railroad that had become the country's leading user of diesels, had been operating its diesel passenger and switching power for years, had the experimental 103 on its property for a month, and stood to be a big customer in the future. When the first Model F rolled out of the La Grange factory, it must have had the Santa Fe's fingerprints all over it.

The minutes don't say what sort of fleet of Model Fs the board envisioned in the summer of 1940. That only two locomotives were being ordered the first time out suggested the Santa Fe wasn't about to dash headlong into freight dieselization, however tempting those internal-combustion machines might look. The first two locomotives would have to prove themselves. Which, of course, they did. Down the road, motive-power studies would propose a larger fleet of FTs than the Santa Fe ultimately bought—as many as 98 of them, when Santa Fe acquired 80.

The Test Department had published its report on the performance of the FT only six weeks before Santa Fe's first order. Behind the scenes, the Santa Fe was already beginning to taste the freight diesel. Division superintendents on the Eastern Lines were instructed to determine what savings in train-miles would be possible if sufficient locomotives like the 103 were available to handle the existing hot Red Ball schedules between Chicago and Wellington. They were asked to redispatch on paper the Red Ball traffic, and then all the traffic, of January 1940.

The superintendents were asked how many locomotives would be required. Six 5,400-horsepower locomotives would do the job on the Middle Division, the study reported. Had train schedules permitted the locomotives to be doubled back within 24 hours, fewer than six would suffice. Each month, 50 fewer trains would be needed. The division suggested that three units, rather than four, could handle the trains.

Similar studies apparently weren't made on the Western Lines west of Wellington or on the Coast Lines west of Belen. It looked as if the new diesels were being considered only as Eastern Lines' power.

Considerable figuring and refiguring would take place, even after the first two locomotives had been delivered, as operating and mechanical experts determined what the gear ratios and top speeds should be, and thus what sort of tonnage they could be expected to handle and how fast they could go with it.

However the new diesels would be used, on September 10, 1940, Santa Fe ordered four two-section Model F freight locomotives. The Santa Fe was going to do what no other railroad had committed itself to do.

Electro-Motive had sold its freight diesel! The Santa Fe had a new Model 100 class!

Given the announced top speeds of those first locomotives, the Santa Fe was going to become a fast-freight railroad, or so said the publicity. But before long it had become clear the new diesels wouldn't be going into high-speed transcontinental freight service. Big, widely appreciated problems lying in wait for the diesels in Arizona and California would make such assignments unlikely.

And while the publicity spoke of faster trains and thus better service, the Santa Fe had as a pragmatic objective reducing the costs of freight train operations. Even on so relatively well-heeled a railroad as the Santa Fe, operating expenses were always a concern.

Some early trade-magazine reports had it right: Santa Fe was acquiring four 2,700-horsepower locomotives. The first eight units were ordered and road-numbered that way. That description quickly disappeared, however. Soon, all official comments referred to two four-unit locomotives that generated 5,400 horsepower each.

A 1988 visit to EMD to research traces of the Santa Fe's 100s yielded just one slim file of value in the room known as Central Files, upstairs over the erecting floor. The file covered order E-351 for the four cab units of the first two locomotives. Long before, it had contained many more documents. However, the few papers still in the manila folder were sufficient to begin to rebuild the history of Santa Fe's freight diesel fleet.

Not to belabor or resolve the issue of whether those locomotives were called FTs or Model Fs or something else, the file called them Model Fs. This was the file of Electro-Motive's Engineering Department, most likely where the "E" prefix to EMD's locomotive order numbers came from.

Electro-Motive began to build Santa Fe's locomotives immediately. Work was initiated by the same sort of engineering release that had gotten the 103 underway. Since the release was dated September 11, 1940, the day after Santa Fe had entered its order, it's evident many conferences between railroad and manufacturer had already taken place.

This is how the document read:

"This release file (although not officially released by Sales) is being established to permit the Engineering Department to release material special for this customer that is not necessarily releasable on Model F Standard. Where Model F is released in one file for both sections, this job will be released as A and B sections separately. See E-352 for B section."

Thus, right from its first internal authority, the Santa Fe would ensure that its individuality—along with test recommendations—would prompt Electro-Motive to produce a different machine from the one demonstrated across the country. It would be Santa Fe's own variation on a mass-produced freight locomotive.

Looking back at Electro-Motive's early meeting with Santa Fe's Mechanical Department managers who balked at the idea of standardization, one wonders about the content of those rolled-up drawings.

To be sure, the two locomotives each would be a combination of four 1,350-horsepower car bodies, two with cabs and two without. But rather than permanently coupled together, the cab and booster car bodies—we introduce them here as "units," not as "sections"—would be entirely separate, one from the other. Both would be completely enclosed. Both would contain batteries. The booster units would have rudimentary controls with which a hostler could run them. The cab and booster units would be fastened together not with permanent drawbars or links but with National Malleable AAR type E couplers—odd couplers, but couplers nonetheless.

Electro-Motive had planned that a two-section 2,700-horsepower combination would be its standard freight locomotive. Its first—and as it would develop, its best—customer had something else in mind. A major recommendation of Santa Fe's Test Department had come into play: the 100s would be composed of individual free-standing units.

The Santa Fe's locomotives would ride on wheels 40 inches in diameter, despite the Test Department's push for at least 50 inches. The wheels under the 103 had been 36 inches in diameter officially, but we've seen that sometimes they were larger. The railroad's freight diesels, at least the first two of them, would be geared for a maximum speed of 80 miles an hour.

Each unit would carry 1,200 gallons of fuel, as had the units of Electro-Motive's 103. Each would carry 245 gallons of radiator water. Lead units, those with cabs, would have room for 22 cubic feet of sand. Trailing units, those without cabs, would have 18.

The mechanisms by which the diesel prime movers would be cooled would be the same as in the 103, except that manually operated friction clutches in the drive trains would permit the fans to be disconnected and stopped, again a Santa Fe recommendation. Not until its last order would automatic controls show up on the radiator shutters—out of the factory, anyway. Some if not all of the 100s assigned for a time to passenger service had automatic shutter controls applied to them by the railroad.

Out of the factory, none of the Santa Fe's locomotives in later orders except for one would contain steam generators. The locomotives that ran for a time in passenger service would be fitted with them as they were prepared for their new assignments.

Santa Fe's requirement that its Model Fs be "units" rather than "sections" had given Electro-Motive something to think about. No such modification had been contemplated in the original Standard design. Placing the trucks beneath the interior ends of a two-section Standard locomotive—almost out to the ends of the units—made it impossible to install couplers at those locations. Electro-Motive had to devise couplers with "gooseneck" shanks that curled up over the tops of the traction motors. Attaching those special couplers to the car bodies would require modifying the frames' end platforms. Down the road, compact draft gear would be developed and put into use in other railroads' FTs, but the gooseneck couplers stayed in the Santa Fe's Model Fs as long as they were in service.

The contour and cross section of those gooseneck shanks might make one wonder about their strength, and about whether the couplers would tend to jackknife. Ultimately, the Santa Fe resolved this issue with stop blocks on either side of the coupler shank, devices that resulted from tests on another railroad. There's no known record of any of the couplers breaking.

In time, Electro-Motive would make available modification kits that would turn dependent FT sections into independent

FT 100 is ready to depart Chicago's Dearborn Station on February 3, 1941, with a demonstration train to Santa Fe's diesel facilities and Electro-Motive's plant in La Grange. *Photo Santa Fe Railway,* Trains *magazine, Kalmbach Media*

units, completely enclosed, with batteries in the B units. Several railroads would install them.

A flurry of orders, drawings, and other documentation quickly differentiated further the Santa Fe's locomotives from Electro-Motive's 103. It must have been a busy time at La Grange for the small engineering staff assigned to the freight locomotive project.

Orders were issued for diaphragms and buffer arrangements, controlled-slack couplers and centering devices, uncoupling gear, fully closed end treatments, end doors, steps and grab irons, and the other parts necessary to complete as units locomotives that had been designed as sections. The file for the B unit would have shown similar changes, plus the addition of batteries and all that went with them.

Section was Electro-Motive's usual term, but some early blueprints used neither *sections* nor *units* to describe the two halves of a Santa Fe Model F. Instead, they were called *cars*.

A release dated October 10, 1940, authorized the purchase of "two triple sash frame number boxes and six glass for number box for each section" from headlight and hardware manufacturer Adams & Westlake. The manufacturer had quoted $86.46 for each sash frame and had promised delivery three weeks from the date of purchase. The illuminated numbers would go on the sides of the cab units, below the windows.

An EMC order 12 days later specified that the side numbers would substitute for the numbers behind the classification lights in the nose. The glass in the nose assemblies was to be painted the locomotive's blue body color. Sockets and bulbs were to be omitted.

Then, 12 days before the 100 was to be delivered, instructions went out to furnish and apply "number-box slide holders" inside the units. The slides could be lowered to hide the numbers in the Adams & Westlake frames. Someone had tumbled to a possible need to do that, evidently. The day would come, though, when the entire fleet would have illuminated road numbers applied behind the classification lights. But first, there was some strenuous work that needed to be done in the field of labor relations.

As was necessary to avoid Illinois state sales tax, upon their completion the first two units of the first locomotive, still the property of Electro-Motive, were moved dead-in-tow by a freight train from McCook, behind the EMC plant, to Shopton, Iowa, adjacent to the division point of Fort Madison. The date was December 30, 1940.

Although it likely didn't happen this way, it's worth imagining—given the historic nature of the occasion—that a Santa Fe guy had been there to hand an Electro-Motive representative a voucher for $247,870.53, maybe with a little ceremony, perhaps a band playing in the background and news reporters gathered 'round. Then the Santa Fe would have owned the first commercial diesel-electric freight locomotive built by Electro-Motive. Half of it, anyway.

The two units were soon on their way to Topeka to be weighed. Their weights would help determine how much their engineers and firemen would be paid.

The cab unit was numbered 100. The trailing or booster unit was numbered 100A. The other half of the first locomotive came along right after the new year began. Carrying road numbers 101 and 101A, it was delivered to McCook on January 2, 1941, then moved dead-in-tow to Shopton. The units went into service there on January 3, en route to Argentine to link up with the 100 and 100A.

But before that, as had been done with the first half of the locomotive, the 101 and 101A were "set up" at Shopton, equipped with the tools and spares they would carry along: rerailing frogs, jacks, air-brake and coupler parts, lamps, fuses, the kinds of things that might be needed quickly and almost impossible to come by on the railroad. A test run awaited the new locomotive. The first outing of the 100, 100A, 101, and 101A pulled a 2,000-ton train to San Bernardino and back.

The 100 already belonged to the Santa Fe, but it wasn't until January 17, 1941, that the formal Authority for Expenditure for the locomotive was signed so the funds were officially available. One wonders if the absence of notoriety about the true first run to California of the 100 was because the Santa Fe wanted to be certain the darn thing would live up to its advance billing before the railroad's public-relations forces uncased their trumpets.

Members of the Chicago Traffic Club inspect the 100 from the tracks of Dearborn Station before departing for the Santa Fe's new diesel shop at 21st Street. *Photo Santa Fe Railway, Barriger National Railroad Library, St. Louis Mercantile Library at University of Missouri-St. Louis*

Facing, During the 100's first runs, Electro-Motive's Dick Dilworth (left) points out a feature of the engine room to Santa Fe's John Morris. *Photo Santa Fe Railway,* Trains *magazine, Kalmbach Media*

Above, Well on its way west during its first run, the 100 takes on fuel from a tank car at Shopton at Fort Madison, Iowa. *Photo Santa Fe Railway, Barriger National Railroad Library, St. Louis Mercantile Library at University of Missouri-St. Louis*

The trumpets did come out early in February, putting on quite a show.

A long advance memo from Lee Lyles, head of the public-relations department, outlined for company officers what was planned. Cosponsoring the festivities would be Volney B. Fowler, public-relations chief of Electro-Motive. The series of events was designed to put the first of the Santa Fe's freight diesels firmly in the minds of editors, reporters, shippers, politicians, and the general public. For a lawyer, Lyles did a fine public-relations job.

On the morning of February 3, 1941, the 100 led a special train out of Chicago's Dearborn Station to the passenger yard at 18th Street so its guests could visit the nearby diesel shop built in 1939. Then it went on to the Electro-Motive plant in La Grange, to be taken back inside the factory for a suitable ceremony. Among the invited were 600 members of the Chicago Traffic Club, the

STREAMLINED FREIGHT TRAINS

Editor's note: The following is a news story from the February 5, 1941, edition of the Topeka (Kansas) Daily Capital:

Topeka gets its first glimpse of the Santa Fe's new diesel-electric freight locomotive today. The two streamlined monsters are to be put into immediate service heading long trains back and forth across the great west. They are the latest word in rapid transportation, and a new step toward overcoming the competition of trucks and airplanes.

The western railroads were first to inaugurate streamlined passenger trains, now regular equipment on most of the trunk lines. The modern demand for speed has revolutionized rail service, and, keeping pace with the times, the Santa Fe went to great expense in streamlining its passenger equipment. The introduction of diesel-electric service to hauling freight is going to shorten the time required for delivery of perishable goods.

These new locomotives have a top cruising speed of 75 miles an hour, can run for long periods without servicing, and have numerous features which make them more efficient than steam power units. It will be an innovation to see long freight trains being yanked across the country at passenger-train speed. But if the Santa Fe's experiment proves successful, which it will, other railroad systems soon will be streamlining their freight trains and then the highways and airways had better look to their laurels.

It is problematic just how much modernization of equipment has affected the overall business of the railroads. Volume of traffic last year was greater than in any year since 1931, with profits rising steadily. The roads have a long way to go before reaching the pre-depression year of 1929, but inauguration of fast passenger and freight service is overcoming the loss of volume to the trucks.

While diesel-electric locomotives have been used in freight yards for several years, the Santa Fe is the first to test them in long-distance hauling. Preliminary tests proved their efficiency and from today on they will be used regularly. Within a few years the old steam locomotive, long the "king" of the freight service, may be relegated to the junkyard.

Facing, The 100 and historic 2-8-0 No. 2414 pose at Topeka with John Purcell, the railroad's longtime chief mechanical officer. *Photo Santa Fe Railway,* Trains *magazine, Kalmbach Media*

Junior Traffic Club, and the Women's Traffic Club. The special was back in Chicago that afternoon.

Carefully timed with the excursion, the US mail delivered information packets across Santa Fe's territory. Editors of newspapers and industry journals were reading a lengthy news release and studying a technical specification sheet about the new locomotive. The publicity pegged February 4 as the date the new locomotive would first go into service.

Many publications received papier-mâché matrices into which had been pressed a screened engraving of the 100. The "mats" could be used to cast type-metal cuts for publication. The photo showed the 100 on the train that had made the earlier run to California. Very likely it was photographed just east of Wellington, as had been EMC's 103.

The next day, February 4, the 100-powered No. 43, the *Northern California Fast Freight,* departed for Shopton. Behind the

Facing, The Texas Panhandle town of Pampa turns out in force to see the 100 during its first trip west. *Photo Santa Fe Railway, Trains magazine, Kalmbach Media*

Above, At Gallup, New Mexico, members of the Taos tribe christen the 100 as the "Lightning Wagon." *Photo Santa Fe Railway, Trains magazine, Kalmbach Media*

engine were five business cars: the 17, 21, 33, 34, and 32, in that order, for the newsmen, dignitaries, railroad officers, and others who were aboard. At Shopton, the car of diesel fuel was placed a cautionary five cars behind the 32. Then the train went on to Argentine.

The business cars stayed at Argentine. A 2-class trailing unit was behind the 100 to provide steam for heat. Dynamometer car 29 came back from Topeka so the test crew members could connect a phone line between the car and the locomotive and then set up their instruments.

That evening, the special left Argentine for California. Its train was Second 43D, again a *Northern California Fast Freight*. An extra was run on 43's regular schedule to get the regular freight-forwarder cars to Amarillo. The special's train was carefully designed. It consisted only of California loads, no more than 70 cars, no more than 2,900 tons. That way, given state laws and the provisions of labor agreements out west, the only switching necessary en route would be to swap way cars.

The publicity train was scheduled to depart Argentine at 8:30 p.m. It was to be at Wellington at 4:30 a.m. February 6, Belen at 6:00 a.m. February 7, and Barstow at 9:00 a.m. February 8. Arrival at Los Angeles was set for 3:00 p.m. Saturday, February 8. The 100 would be fueled at Wellington and probably at Clovis, Belen, or Barstow. Emporia would be ready to water the units, if necessary, handling the train as it had handled Electro-Motive's experimental 103 and its train. A yard engine would take the outgoing engine crew to the yard from the roundhouse and bring the incoming crew back.

Between the business cars and the car of diesel fuel were two cars of Studebaker bodies, a car of engines for North American Aviation, a car of meat for John Morrell & Co., and a car of automobile parts from Fisher Body in Memphis. Behind the car of fuel were cars of freight-forwarder traffic, tile, tires, auto bodies, canned goods, automobiles, merchandise, more forwarder traffic, radios, more merchandise, flour, furniture, sugar, aluminum machinery, more automobiles, more machinery, steel plates, and, out of Argentine, way car 1717.

En route west, the 100 paused for public visitations at Barstow, Pampa, and Amarillo. It stopped at Gallup for a notable ceremony: Native Americans of the Pueblo and Navajo tribes christened Santa Fe's 100 "Lightning Wagon" in the Navajo tongue.

Famous western personages were on hand at Gallup to help introduce the 100, according to the *Gallup Independent*. Henry Chee Dodge, venerable former Navajo war chief, was there; as were Navajo Chief Many Goats and his brother Gambler; and Taos dancers White Eagle, Deer Leader, Deer Followers, and Talking Water. On hand were John Wetherill, Indian trader and one of the discoverers of Mesa Verde; and Roman Hubbell, operator of Navajo Tours. The festivities at Gallup took all of 15 minutes, and then the 100 was again underway.

Some news media representatives from on-line points got the chance to make part of the trip. For example, the publishers of the two Gallup newspapers were aboard from Gallup to Winslow.

Lyles wanted to have the 100 photographed with a 5001-class 2-10-4, which meant that somewhere on the Southern District the photo would have to be set up, and the publicity train might be delayed. "It may be necessary to hold up departure Belen until there is sufficient daylight to take photographs, in which case it is understood that such delays will be overcome and on-time arrival at Barstow accomplished," one message about the trip said. The photo ultimately was made at Clovis. It showed the 100 sandwiched between two of the Santa Fe's best steam locomotives, 2-10-4 No. 5006 and 4-8-4 No. 2908.

Diesel Power magazine's correspondent was clearly excited by the publicity run. He provided his readers with considerable detail about the 100's performance:

"Not since the original Burlington *Zephyr* started its first test run as America's first diesel railroad passenger train six years ago has there been another 'grade A' diesel landmark," reported the April 1941 issue.

February 4 and 5, the world's first main-line diesel freight locomotive began its westward trip at the head end of a 3,000-ton freight train, over the Santa Fe system between Chicago and Los Angeles. The last part of a three-cornered chapter in the dieselization of American railroads was completed at Los Angeles February 8 when the big EMD locomotive, with its

A guest on the exhibition run—likely a newspaper reporter—enjoys a game of solitaire in the business car. *Photo Santa Fe Railway,* Trains *magazine, Kalmbach Media*

four 1,350-horsepower units clicking like the proverbial Swiss watch, rolled to a stop just 72 hours out from Argentine Yard, Kansas City, 1,782 miles away, and boasting of a record running time of 55 hours, the difference being consumed by side trips to Topeka and many stops to let local people inspect the latest diesel creation.

The magazine reported that on grades the 100's drawbar pull approached 200,000 pounds, well over the maximum a steam locomotive could produce. Somewhere on the trip, a piston or cylinder liner failed, and one of the four units was shut down for several hours for repairs. Still, the train made its schedule. At another point, when the train was on three sharp curves and

A Big Coming-out Party

Facing, In a view from the cupola of the dynamometer car, the 100 and its exhibition train head west toward California. *Photo Santa Fe Railway,* Trains *magazine, Kalmbach Media*

Above, Heading up a specially arranged publicity freight train, the 100 poses in Cajon Pass during the first trip west. *Photo Santa Fe Railway, Wallace W. Abbey Collection*

Above, The 100 and an abbreviated exhibition train arrive at San Diego's elegant Mission-style depot on February 11, 1941. *Photo Santa Fe Railway, Trains magazine, Kalmbach Media*

Facing, Visitors surround the 100 during its display at Santa Fe's Redondo Junction roundhouse in Los Angeles. *Photo Santa Fe Railway, Trains magazine, Kalmbach Media*

its rear end was out of sight, the brakes were applied from the way car. The locomotive was dragged to a stop. "The enormous load almost pulled three drawbars, but not even a wheel slip was noticed," according to its story.

Except for the one unit, the locomotive was not shut down anywhere on the run. "Rarely did the hot engine alarm sound, nor did any other failure except the damaged liner develop worth noting. The engine ran at constant speed with no auxiliary trouble of any kind other than a plugging of an oil filter."

Diesel Power compared favorably the typical 12- to 14-miles-per-hour speed of a 60-car steam-powered train with the faster 22 to 27 miles an hour of the 100:

"Downhill, due to the sensationally perfect performance of the regenerative braking system or dynamic brakes, as Electro-Motive calls them now, a speed of close to 25 miles per hour was maintained, with no stops to cool the brake shoes off. On four sections of the line, averaging 20 miles each in total distance, or a total of 83 miles, the new braking system was successfully used. Cool brake shoes, no ruined treads on boxcar wheels, elimination of flat wheels and heat damage, faster operation downhill, and no long stops to cool wheels were the advantages."

The 100's dynamic brake was used for the 40 miles between Mountainair and Belen, the 23 miles between Louise and Yucca, the 19 miles from Supai to Ash Fork, and the 22.5 miles from Summit to San Bernardino.

According to the magazine, the dynamic brakes reduced the usual number of air-brake applications by three-fourths. Never did the temperatures of locomotive or car wheels exceed 130 degrees, which it called "a trifle hotter" than sun temperature.

"Normally, a freight run between Chicago and Los Angeles would involve nine locomotives and would stop 34 to 36 times for fuel and water," the magazine reported. The diesel test run, with the same load, used but one locomotive and made only five routine stops for fuel and water. "Comparative operation over the entire run with nine steam locomotives would raise the fuel cost for oil and coal to approximately $1,100." Figures accompanying the story showed that fuel for the 100 averaged four cents per gallon and that 4,400 gallons were used.

Fewer than 700 gallons of water were supplied to the locomotive en route. Steam locomotives would have consumed 750,000 gallons. "On the Santa Fe," *Diesel Power* concluded, "there are 1,200 miles of route where water supply is almost as costly as fuel."

San Diego was next on the list of places the 100 visited. It was on public display there on February 11. Its Los Angeles debut took place February 13. It left San Bernardino headed east on February 16, towing the dynamometer car, two business cars, and the fuel car. John Morris had instructed that it lead a train of 2,700 tons of as many through loads as possible. A helper would be necessary from San Bernardino to Summit and from Ash Fork to Supai. The train could be filled out at Gallup, once it was clear of Arizona's train limit.

Before it went back east, the 100 was taken up to Cajon Pass for photographs, including from the air, with a train headed by newly painted refrigerator cars and boxcars. A shot of the train on what in later years would be named Sullivan's Curve was widely publicized as having been made on the "first eastbound run." But no dynamometer car, fuel car, or business cars are visible behind the engine. It must have been a public-relations setup.

Perhaps some refreshed publicity was needed, to clarify why a few weeks after the 100, 100A, 101A, and 101 had been sent off to California, their road numbers had already changed. Shopton revised the units to 100, 100A, 100B, and 100C.

On the run to California, the illuminated number panels of the sides of the trailing unit, which would have shown it to have been the 101, had displayed no number at all. The dark slides were firmly in place.

The second locomotive ordered in September 1940 was delivered the following March. It, too, had cab units at each end. Its units originally were to have been numbered 102, 102A, 103A, and 103. Before they left La Grange, Santa Fe instructed Electro-Motive to number them 101, 101A, 101B, and 101C.

While road numbers of the initial 100 class of freight diesels might have shuffled around, the locomotives did anything but. Soon, the 100 and 101 were placed into regular revenue service. Two more 5,400-horsepower diesel locomotives were ordered in early March 1941. Santa Fe was now well on its way to what its publicity department called "the largest fleet of diesel power in service on any railroad in the world."

On one of its early trips, the 100 gives local crews a taste of diesel railroading, at the engine terminal at Shopton, Iowa. *Photo Santa Fe Railway, Barriger National Railroad Library, St. Louis Mercantile Library at University of Missouri-St. Louis*

Powered by Electro-Motive 567 engines, navy LST ships unload troops in the Philippines in the Battle of Leyte in late 1944. *US Landing Ship Tank Association Collection, National Archives*

TEN ELECTRO-MOTIVE GOES TO WAR

A Locomotive Builder Serves the US Navy

THE YEAR 1939 WAS PIVOTAL IN AMERICAN RAILROAD HIStory. Early that year, on February 1, Electro-Motive's engineering release began the birth of the FT diesel engine. Seven months later, on September 1, the nation saw the beginning of World War II.

At dawn that autumn morning, without provocation, without warning, planes of the German Luftwaffe dove out of the sky over the Polish fishing village of Puck and attacked the community and its air base.

Although it would be another two months before Electro-Motive's prototype 103 would leave the factory, a huge task already was taking shape for the Santa Fe's first diesel-electric freight locomotives. The railroad would be called upon to move millions of pieces of machinery to the coasts of the United States, destined for war theaters east and west. Passenger trains, too, would move millions of troops.

In 1939, the railroad industry was composed of more than a hundred major and a great many relatively minor companies that together operated 45,000 locomotives, 1.6 million freight cars, and 39,000 passenger cars over 235,000 miles of track. These railroads would play major roles in the war effort, perhaps none as large as the Santa Fe's.

By late 1939, railroads could feel the beginning of the defense buildup. For the Santa Fe, the Model F freight diesel could not come out of La Grange soon enough.

As essential as Electro-Motive was to the Santa Fe during the war, it had another pressing customer: the US Navy. From the vantage point of EMC's parent company, General Motors, World War II had begun years earlier when the navy first came to call. At the time, with very few boats in the water powered by domestic engines, the navy sought out GM Research Labs and competitor Fairbanks-Morse for a lightweight diesel.

As evidence of its strategic planning in the prewar years, the government envisioned needing to deliver heavy tanks in great numbers to battlefields across considerable distances—across oceans, even. The caterpillar-tread tank would be an essential tool of war.

The navy in 1935 began to design oceangoing ships that could land these tanks, troops, and supplies on enemy-held beaches. It needed a new engine for these craft, as well as one for its growing fleet of ships used as submarine chasers. The result was General Motors' long research and development project, out of which came a progression of diesel engines tailored for naval use: the 201A, the 184, and the 567. Electro-Motive was increasingly involved in this effort.

The 201A went into navy craft until the Model 184 was ready. Nicknamed the Quad, the 201A consisted of four GM 6-71 truck and bus diesels geared to a bull ring. Together, the four engines kicked out 1,800 horsepower. Two Quads would produce the power a sub chaser required.

Thirty-five hundred copies of the Quad were produced for a vessel that GM once described as "a clinker-built boat forward, a Japanese sampan amidships, and a Kanawha River mud boat aft." Dick Dilworth didn't think much of the gearboxes and

A VISIT TO THE WAR PRODUCTION BOARD

Editor's note: In 1949, Electro-Motive's Harold Hamilton spoke to the Pacific Railway Club and offered the following:

You probably remember that at the time of the war there were a lot of people in Washington assigned to look over industry as a whole to find out what industries did, how important they were to the war effort, to national defense—and they had a big red pencil and the important thing was to decide when an industry was not essential.

The War Production Board had just been established. Mr. Ralph Budd, who was president of the Burlington and one of the original members of the War Production Board, called me on the phone from Washington and asked, "What are you doing to establish in the minds of the people in Washington the importance of the diesel locomotive?"

I said, "Nothing."

He said, "It's about time you did something."

So, I went to Washington. I found that the man who had been assigned the job of deciding what locomotives and rolling stock and things of that kind were essential, not knowing about diesel locomotives, had gone to the *Encyclopedia Britannica*. He found an article written in 1934 at the time the first streamlined locomotives were put in service—and it was true, the first two had been exhibited at the [1933–1934 World's] Fair in Chicago and also in the more important cities of America—anyway, the encyclopedia simply stated that a diesel locomotive consisted of "a car mounted on railroad trucks, in which an engine, generators, and necessary appurtenances are included, which is used to pull gaily colored trains for exhibition purposes."

The diesel locomotive was classified as nonessential.

All we had to do was spread the word among the railroad people, who did the rest. The net result was an early change in the program to make the diesel locomotive, particularly for switching service, essential, and it was given a relatively high rating. Manufacturers made diesels to the full extent of their capabilities throughout the war period.

---

clutches that synchronized the Quad's engines, but he had to admit they worked.

The first pilot model of the 16-cylinder 184 "pancake" diesel, a joint project of Electro-Motive and fellow GM subsidiary Detroit Diesel, was tested on October 11, 1941. It was a stack of four "layers," each containing four radially arranged cylinders, all on their sides, cranking a central drive shaft. The 184 gave a sub chaser twice the capability of the gasoline-powered boats of World War I without gasoline's explosive personality. It developed 1,200 horsepower at 1,800 revolutions per minute and weighed a fifth of a 12-cylinder 567.

The navy accepted the 184 on February 4, 1942. Electro-Motive engineers and service personnel helped install two 184s in an experimental 110-foot sub chaser, the wooden hull of which was built by GM subsidiary Fisher Body. It was commissioned on March 18, 1942.

Facing, As the end of World War II approaches, a fleet of FT diesels congregates at the roundhouse in Winslow, Arizona, in April 1945. *Photo Santa Fe Railway, Stan Kistler Collection*

Above and facing, Santa Fe advertisements promote the railroad's war effort. *Photos Santa Fe Railway, Wallace W. Abbey Collection*

The 201A essentially was retired once the 184 was accepted. The navy ordered 100 engines along with propellers, shafts, and other parts. As enemy submarines torpedoed Allied ships at an alarming rate and new sub-chaser hulls waited for engines, more and larger orders from the navy followed. Electro-Motive soon took over the engineering aspects of the 184 program. Research Labs personnel moved from Detroit to La Grange. The navy set up a resident inspector of machinery at the EMD factory.

The navy was becoming Electro-Motive's biggest customer. In conjunction with the British Admiralty, the navy in the late 1930s had designed what would be called the LST, the Landing Ship, Tank, a giant vessel capable of transiting the ocean carrying several tanks as well as soldiers and supplies.

To show the navy what the 567 could do, Electro-Motive pulled an engine out of locomotive production and ran it non-stop for 15 hours, producing 960 horsepower at 720 revolutions per minute. Then, without stopping the engine, it stepped up

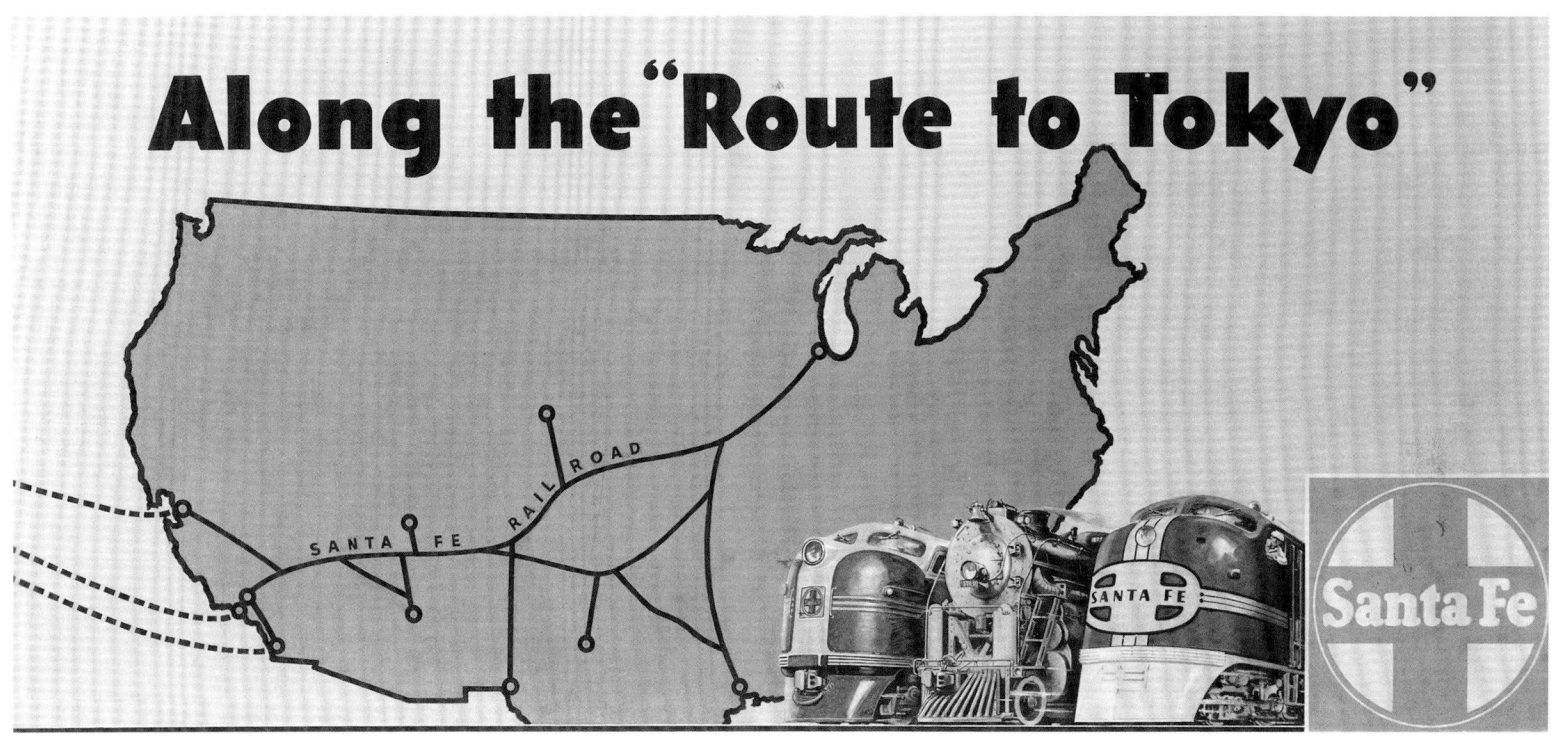

both load and speed and ran the engine for another 2 hours at 800 revolutions per minute, producing 1,200 horsepower. The navy inspector, impressed, looked on.

The LST would use a modified 567 engine, its big blowers mounted inboard to reduce the total width of the engine so it would fit the cramped space in the hull. The modifications were done by Cleveland Diesel Division, formerly Winton.

When Japan attacked Pearl Harbor in December 1941, the LST was one of eight types of oceangoing landing ships still in design.

A year earlier, Electro-Motive and the navy had begun construction on the "Navy Building," a factory addition that would add 121,300 square feet of manufacturing floor space at La Grange. Electro-Motive built the building, and the navy provided the equipment, including an initial batch of 255 machine tools. Fairbanks-Morse got a similar building and American Locomotive Company, which was producing tanks, got some new facilities as well.

The Navy Building, windowless and air-conditioned, was finished in May 1941, more than a year earlier than the delivery of many crucial machine tools, causing production challenges and delays. When Electro-Motive executed its first contract with the navy for Model 184 engines, the schedule called for 10 per month. As war efforts grew, demand doubled. The navy eventually put

Facing, A huge naval gun headed for the West Coast rides flatcars on a Santa Fe freight at Waynoka, Oklahoma, in 1943. *Photo Jack Delano, Prints & Photographs Division, Library of Congress*

Above, In a view from a passing caboose, a Santa Fe freight hauls army tanks in March 1943, somewhere between Seligman, Arizona, and Needles, California. *Photo Jack Delano, Prints & Photographs Division, Library of Congress*

Wartime commodity: a four-unit FT diesel set rolls through a reverse curve in Arizona with a trainload of crude oil. *Photo Santa Fe Railway, Stan Kistler Collection*

664 machine tools, used for some 600 different production parts, into La Grange. Electro-Motive kept up its production of 20 engines a month until May 1944, when the navy contract ended.

While Electro-Motive was managing its engine production, the Santa Fe was adjusting to its growing freight traffic. The pace of the war increased so quickly that suddenly tracks were full of trains. There was no way for construction gangs to get in to increase track capacity—if the material with which to do so were available, which it usually was not.

Docks across North American port cities, too, were crammed. The congestion wasn't the railroads' fault; they were delivering to the ports faster than the ports were loading ships and getting them back to sea.

Even before Pearl Harbor, the Santa Fe's and other railroads' yards at Albuquerque, Spokane, Salt Lake City, Ogden, El Paso, Auburn, and other stations well back in the interior had become staging areas for export shipments. Government traffic was held there until destination ports were able to handle it. Contractors used idle freight cars essentially as storage lockers, adding to railroad bottlenecks.

The problem of port congestion would recur throughout the war. Pacific coast ports, for example, had been designed mainly to unload incoming ships. Dockworkers found it very difficult to efficiently unload railcars and fill ships bound for destinations overseas.

The Santa Fe and other railroads faced myriad challenges during these years. The vulnerability of American oil tankers to enemy submarines off the East Coast, for instance, moved oil traffic inland, to rail. Trains of tank cars originated in Louisiana, Mississippi, Texas, Oklahoma, and Kansas, bound for East Coast refineries. Coming up out of the Gulf coast states, these trains would turn not only east, but west. There was high demand for oil in West Coast states too.

The military's own traffic was massive. To move a fully equipped army division took not only the necessary passenger cars but approximately 1,000 freight cars. In the 45 months from December 1941 to August 1945, more than 33 million troops moved by rail. War-related railroad freight totaled 294 million tons. The Santa Fe received its fair share.

The bureau of ships had advised Electro-Motive to give its undivided attention to the navy landing craft programs. Still, there is nothing to suggest that EMD stopped producing locomotives altogether during the war. The lack of machine tools in 1943 brought locomotive production to a standstill for two months, but La Grange made up for lost time.

Even when the navy work was at its peak, EMD squeezed out one four-section FT for the Southern, two for the Rio Grande, and seven for the Santa Fe. All told, Electro-Motive's production for the railroad industry during the war years included 139 switchers, 280 Model F units or sections, and 30 streamliner passenger units.

Moreover, by early 1943, an improved successor to the Model F was appearing on Electro-Motive's drafting boards. Even as they were learning much about the performance of the FT, designers were holding back improvements and refinements during the war. Demand was sure to be large, postwar.

Some say the Allies won World War II on the strength of the productive capacity of the United States—300,000 warplanes; 124,000 ships of all types; 41 billion rounds of ammunition; 100,000 tanks and armored cars; 2.4 million military trucks; 434 million tons of steel; 36 billion yards of cotton textiles; oil, copper, guns of all kinds—over five years.

All that war material had to be delivered to where it was needed, safely and with speed. Getting it started on its way was what American railroads like the Santa Fe did and, considering the circumstances, did well indeed.

ELEVEN THE UNIONS AND THE LAWS

The Challenges to Operating Efficiency

THE SANTA FE'S MANY CONSTITUENCIES—INCLUDING ITS employees, labor unions, and state and federal governments—had settled over 40 years into the traditions and norms of steam-powered freight. Electro-Motive's experimental 103 diesel-electric upended many established patterns and rules. The advent of the 103 created not only the potential for great efficiency but also for great conflict. Change has a way of doing that.

Consider a virtual concentric circle of Santa Fe's various constituents, hovering and spinning—usually relentlessly—over the desks of management and over the tables in wood-paneled boardrooms. In the innermost ring of this circle of impending change, closest to home, were the railroad's employees.

From the moment the olive-and-gold 103 dropped down off the Arizona Divide and stopped at Seligman to change crews, it was evident opinions differed about this new form of motive power. Seligman was a terminal and railroad shop town, a livestock-shipping station, and little else. The existence and livelihood of much of Seligman depended on the steam locomotive. Most of the citizenry stood on the depot platform to look at this new diesel. Few greeted it with a smile.

Historically, railroads weren't prone to precipitous change. But now, the very rate of change had increased. The chance to work a full and fruitful career on a locomotive was jeopardized. In the cab, the diesel-electric would require, immediately, new engineering skills. The roles of the fireman and the maintainer were in question. On the road, fewer stops meant reduced crews. In the yard and the shops, the impact was also apt to be profound—especially as the diesels began to proliferate.

Longtime railroaders at Seligman and across the Santa Fe property were dizzy with questions and uncertainty about job security, working environment, crew sizes, wage calculations, and more.

For answers, for support, and for leadership in whatever fights were to come, the operating crafts—engineers, firemen, conductors, brakemen, and switchmen—turned, as always, to their labor unions. So did the shop crafts.

As negotiators on behalf of their members, union leaders were influential in power. Across the railroad industry were at least two dozen unions. The four largest were the Brotherhood of Locomotive Engineers, formed in 1867; the Order of Railway Conductors, 1868; the Brotherhood of Locomotive Firemen and Engineers, 1873; and the Brotherhood of Railroad Trainmen, 1883. They were known, not surprisingly, as the brotherhood.

Since their inception, the unions' primary strategy was to push for more and better jobs, predetermined and narrowly defined. Disputes over the specificity and scope of work rules marked the vast majority of labor/management confrontations. The Santa Fe and other railroads found it hard to fight back against the

Facing, The head brakeman looks back over his train as it rolls west through Johnson Canyon, between Williams and Ash Fork, Arizona. *Photo Jack Delano, Prints & Photographs Division, Library of Congress*

STRING OF HORSEPOWERS

Editor's note: The following is testimony of Electro-Motive's Richard M. Dilworth, chief engineer, in his appearance before the Emergency Board, First Diesel Case, Chicago, 1943:

Richard M. Dilworth.
Trains *magazine, Kalmbach Media*

Sidney S. Alderman, counsel for the western railroads: "Now Mr. Dilworth, in each of the Firemen's case and the Engineers' case, the organization is seeking a change in the basis of pay from weight on drivers to horsepower in the case of the diesel-electric locomotive. From your knowledge as a mechanical engineer, I wish you would give the Board the benefit of your views as to whether horsepower is a proper and practicable pay base upon which to base wages of engine crews."

Dilworth: "That seems to lead to a discussion of horsepower as the measurement of a diesel-electric locomotive. There has been a good deal of talk so far, and it has all been about the horsepower of the diesel engine. The diesel engine is only part of this diesel locomotive.

"It has been said that we talk about horsepower when we are selling the locomotive, and we do. It is a good, convenient handle to use in describing the size of a locomotive. But it is not a very accurate description. You might say that horsepower is a yardstick, but when you talk about the size of a locomotive in terms which will allow the measurement made to be used as a base of pay, there is apt to be a good deal of inaccuracy. In other words, we want to set aside our yardstick and use a micrometer.

"Now, the Firemen have asked that the rate of pay be based on the horsepower as rated by the manufacturer."

Alderman: "With one reservation, Mr. Dilworth. They say that if in any particular instance they can demonstrate that the manufacturer's rating is wrong, they want it corrected."

Dilworth: "Well, they can *always* demonstrate that. The horsepower the manufacturer uses as a rating for the locomotive is that stamped on the nameplate of the diesel engine, and it is only one of many horsepower ratings that could be applied to the locomotive.

"I hate to wander off the subject, but I am afraid I've got to."

Here, Dick Dilworth painted a picture of the Mojave River, how the flow of its water was measured in cubic feet per second, and how that flow varied from Victorville to Barstow and other points along the shore. Diesel horsepower, Dilworth testified, also varied because of many factors. One was tractive effort.

Dilworth: "The locomotive that has been mentioned is this 5,400-horsepower diesel freight locomotive. That is what we talk about, right up to the point when we are going to make the sale. At that point, we begin to talk about something more accurately determinable than the horsepower of the engine. We build into our specifications a chart showing the tractive effort available at the rim of the driving wheels at each speed for which we are selling our locomotive to run.

"We can take the assumption that the engines will each deliver exactly 1,350 horsepower to the generator, the first unit in the electric transmission. We can calculate the losses in the generator, the wiring, the traction motors, and the driving wheels, and arrive at the horsepower and the tractive effort for each speed.

"Or we can take the average efficiency of the electric transmission and subtract it from 5,400 horsepower, which is our rating. That is not so accurate. However, it is the way we do it, and the way we make sales. The difference in accuracy between the long, drawn-out, carefully calculated method and the shortcut is not so great as the uncertainty of the horsepower was to begin with."

At 7.5, 30, and 40 miles an hour and depending on measurement technique, Dilworth laid out, anywhere from 370 to 1,400 horsepower could be lost. He expounded in more detail, then shifted his testimony to the built-in accessories in a diesel engine.

Dilworth: "A diesel engine by itself is kind of a helpless thing. It will not work unless it is surrounded with blowers and pumps. Those parasite losses eat up horsepower. By the time the horsepower comes out to the end of the crankshaft, where it is measurable, there is about—oh, somewhere around 80 percent of what was made in the cylinders. Now, that is where the manufacturer that I work for rated his earliest diesel engines—the horsepower that came out of this shaft. However, maybe there is a word of explanation that would be well."

For perhaps an hour, Dilworth talked about the horsepower drain of attached-to-but-not-built-in accessories, the efficiency of the electric transmission, and the limitations of the dynamometer car.

Dilworth: "Now, if we determine where we are going to measure this river, whether at Victorville, Barstow, or where along the long stretch of loss of horsepower we are going to make our measurement, then we run into trouble again."

Here came another volley of mechanical details and mathematical formulas dealing with torque, speed, and altitude; his testimony bordered on an introductory lecture in physics.

Dilworth: "So coming back to our railroad engine, we add to the 1,479 horsepower, which is the nameplate rating plus the attached accessories, an allowance of about 8 percent for weather conditions. We test an engine here near Chicago at an altitude of about 600 feet above sea level and in a factory where the temperature is kept someplace between 70 and 90 degrees. Under those test conditions, 412 cubic millimeters of fuel will deliver at the engine shaft about 1,595 to 1,610 horsepower. It varies from engine to engine, and we are not very particular about the variation because what we sold was 1,350 horsepower, and we are quite sure we are going to give the customer what he bought.

"But I frankly do not know where, along this string of horsepowers, it would be a practical place to pick one and say that is an accurate determination of the locomotive, sufficiently accurate to use as a basis of wages.

"Does that cover your case?"

Alderman: "I think so."

Instruction material for various series of FT diesels presented a new challenge for steam-age railroaders.
Photo Wallace W. Abbey, Center for Railroad Photography & Art Collection

tide of restrictive rules. Employee strikes were not uncommon; state and federal courts tended to favor the unions. Over time, the Santa Fe had more than once reluctantly agreed to what it viewed as wasteful employment practices.

When in the mid-1930s diesel-electrics began to show up here and there, the brotherhoods had quickly identified them as a threat to jobs. The role of the fireman was an obvious target, prompting the Brotherhood of Locomotive Firemen and Engineers (BofLF&E) in 1936 to demand a fireman on each diesel. The railroads seemed not to object; they agreed to the firemen and their salaries largely because this form of motive power was still widely considered specialized. Railroad management had not yet acknowledged—perhaps had not yet believed themselves—that steam sooner or later would become an anachronism.

By mid-March 1937, railroads whose firemen the BofLF&E represented began filling the positions and considered the matter resolved. The Brotherhood of Locomotive Engineers (BLE) had other ideas. Six months later it served notice on the Santa Fe and five other roads, insisting they modify significantly the agreement they had made with the BofLF&E. The long confrontation that resulted would be known as the First Diesel Case.

After working its demands through local levels according to bargaining protocol long ago established by the Railway Labor Act, the BLE presented a collective national front in October 1939. The union had two central demands, sensing something insidious to its interests was coming in the form of future locomotives. Both demands were aimed at the two-unit and three-unit diesel consists appearing on some passenger streamliners. Since road freight diesels were going into service as negotiations were getting underway, they became part of the case.

The first demand dealt with the calculation of engineers' wages. Since 1919, a fireman and an engineer had been compensated on a scale based on the weight of a locomotive on its driving wheels. Now, 20 years later, the BLE wanted its engineers more highly paid, using a scale based on the horsepower developed by a locomotive's prime mover and guaranteed by its manufacturer.

The second demand was an even bigger issue for the railroads. The BLE wanted one of its members to be employed as an "assistant engineer" in the engine room of each unit of a multiple-unit diesel locomotive. This would include the cab unit in which, of course, an engineer was already employed. The Santa Fe was adamant in its opposition.

By the spring of 1940, Fred Gurley was appointed chair of a railroad executive committee to deal with the demands of the BLE. Not to be outdone, and certainly not to permit members of the BLE to perform firemen's work, or the work of an onboard maintainer out of the shop crafts, the BofLF&E filed notices of its own. In mid-May 1941, Gurley would chair a parallel committee to deal with the new demands of the BofLF&E.

The Firemen's demands followed the pattern of the Engineers': firemen too should be compensated on a graduated scale based on the rated horsepower of the prime mover. And a fireman was to be employed in each unit of the locomotive. In essence, the two unions wanted one man—one man represented by each union, that is—in each unit of the locomotive, whether the unit had a cab or not.

———

By now, the Santa Fe was counting on its fleet of FTs as relief of the high labor costs of its steam locomotives. Inserting its growing number of multiple-unit Model Fs into the scene had immensely complicated the labor picture. Ultimately, the two unions combined their cases in a national dispute. Negotiations were so contentious that in February 1943, President Franklin Roosevelt appointed an Emergency Board to recommend a settlement.

Mountains of testimony and miles of transcript resulted from the hearings. The principal issue was engine-crew size. The stakes were huge. The Engineers still wanted to add an assistant in each unit of the consist; the Firemen insisted on a man in each trailing unit. At least one brakeman would be used in freight service, and the Santa Fe and some other roads specified a maintainer to oversee the power plant. The cost of a potential crew of 11 or 12 on a four-unit locomotive would be prohibitive.

It took only three months, until May 1943, for the Emergency Board to convey its recommendations—denying demands for all additional crew and only modestly adjusting pay—to Roosevelt. It took only three days for the BofLF&E's leader to gain an audience with the president and express the brotherhood's dissatisfaction.

Roosevelt sent the parties back to the bargaining table. When, six months later, an agreement was finally reached, terms varied little from the recommendations of the Emergency Board. The BofLF&E conceded on the manning issue in exchange for a point or two on firemen's wages. The BLE gave up its assistant engineers in exchange for assurance a fireman would not do an engineer's job.

The opening salvo of what became the First Diesel Case had occurred seven years earlier. Still, some grumbled that the orderly process of labor relations had been harmed by political influence, that Roosevelt's intervention undermined the Emergency Board. Be that as it may, at least the Santa Fe could return more of its attention to other labor issues.

———

The doubleheader rule prohibited two locomotives to jointly pull a train of more than 40 cars, exclusive of cabooses, unless the rating of the largest engine handling the train was not exceeded. This contractual agreement was not between the Santa Fe and its engineers or firemen; it was a compromise in 1903 between railroads in the West and the brotherhoods of conductors and trainmen.

The brotherhoods had argued for this safety rule to relieve their members of the burden of watching excessively long and heavy trains in mountainous, curve-ridden territory. To avoid violating the doubleheader rule, railroads could pay double mileage to the one crew or pay for a second crew to ride along. The western carriers argued that the rule artificially limited the tonnage a train crew could handle, but several stabs at eliminating it met without success.

The advent of Electro-Motive's 193-foot-long Model F would put the doubleheader rule to the test. There was no arguing that an out-of-the-catalog four-unit 5,400-horsepower FT, with two cabs, was really two identical 2,700-horsepower locomotives coupled back-to-back. Unless the four units were permanently coupled or only had one cab, a railroad violated the doubleheader rule the moment its train left town.

Most railroads that acquired FTs considered it altogether proper that the four sections be linked with undividable drawbars. Not the Santa Fe, who wanted its 100 class to be as flexible as possible and thus made up of independent units, not dependent sections. The railroad went to some expense to have Electro-Motive modify the units' coupling.

The Santa Fe's 100 and 101 had a cab at each end. Then, the railroad began reconfiguring and renumbering subsequent Model Fs into consists of one lead unit followed by three boosters. Did the railroad do this because of the doubleheader rule? It's plausible. Shortly after the 100 and 101 went into service, some trainmen did file claims based on the tonnage the new diesels were handling.

For all the headaches that 193 feet of undividable FT must have been—for hostlers, dispatchers, and shop foremen—creating with a center drawbar what reasonably could only be called a single locomotive was about all most railroads saddled with the doubleheader rule could do physically to circumvent it. Periodically making and breaking connections between the units was not a practical option. Using jumper cables carried safety risks.

In labor panels and elsewhere, management claimed an FT could not be operated by two engineers manipulating the controls in the two cabs simultaneously. They contended the cab at the nonoperating end was there simply for the convenience of turning the locomotive at the end of its run. These and other rationales had little effect; in the end, the Santa Fe and other railroads could abide by the doubleheader rule or ignore it and take their chances.

State laws added to the complexity of managing the railroads during the time of the FT.

Arizona, the heart of Santa Fe territory, had in place statutes from the early 1900s that put a maximum limit on train size and a minimum on the size of the crew.

In 1912, voters passed a law that required passenger trains to be no more than 14 cars and freight trains no more than 70. Fines would be levied upon each violation. The train-length law hampered the Santa Fe from Gallup to California. Arizona was pressured repeatedly to eliminate this statute, which stood in the way of conducting efficient business. The law survived many state and federal appeals before the US Supreme Court ruled it unconstitutional in 1945.

Many other states in and out of Santa Fe territory had similar laws. Oklahoma and Louisiana, for example, had passed train-size laws in 1939; they bit the dust the same day Arizona's did. Arizona also had a state crew-size law, requiring a third brakeman on all freight trains of 39 cars or more. This statute stood for many years, even though the railroad's agreement with labor unions contained no such provision.

California complicated the crew-size formula, requiring the number of brakemen to be proportionate to train tonnage and

Facing, Engineer George Bertino at the throttle of an FT rolling out of Winslow, Arizona, with wartime tonnage. *Photo Jack Delano, Prints & Photographs Division, Library of Congress*

Facing, In the engine compartment, W. F. Leverenz works as a maintainer, a regular assignment on early FT runs. *Photo Jack Delano, Prints & Photographs Division, Library of Congress*

Right, Inside the B section of an FT, a hostler's control stand includes a throttle and reverser lever. Out of the picture at the top is the air-brake control. *Photo Electro-Motive Division, Wallace W. Abbey Collection*

Facing, Fresh from rebuilding at the San Bernardino shops, an original FT set performs break-in runs as helpers on Cajon Pass. *Richard Steinheimer Photographic Collection, DeGolyer Library, Southern Methodist University*

Above, Service in a hurry: crews attend to FT diesels on the run-through fuel rack at Winslow, Arizona. *Photo Santa Fe Railway, Wallace W. Abbey Collection*

grade. A Santa Fe official once recalled that there were so many brakemen on a freight train, some couldn't find places to sit. This law was repealed in 1948.

The public, in the form of legislators and bureaucrats, were not content to leave railroad labor/management issues to railroad labor and railroad management. Union bosses kept continual pressure not only on the railroads but on state and federal agencies. The brotherhoods were more than happy to have government's help to achieve their goals.

Fred Gurley testified on this issue in 1941: "During the last two decades we have had to oppose about 178 different bills that would have limited and restricted the length of trains. There were 198 different bills that would have forced the use of more men than were actually needed in the operation of freight and passenger trains."

After itemizing more proposed legislation that would have resulted in unnecessary man-hours, impaired efficiency, and reduced productivity, Gurley summed up: "It will be observed that the grand total is about 646 bills."

He then turned his testimony toward a similar avalanche of bills either supported by management but not labor or the other way around. His point was clear: there was more than enough law—enacted and proposed, valid or not—to hamper railroads' ability to do their best business.

The federal government, the Santa Fe's most pervasive constituency, perhaps cared more that railroads did their fairest business than their best business. The Interstate Commerce Commission was established in 1887 to ensure fair rail rates, sniff out any form of discrimination, and oversee the way railroads utilized their car fleets.

The ICC was well aware of state statutes and labor agreements, especially on parts of the Coast Lines, that limited train-car length and outlawed doubleheaders. It knew that rail-service congestion would occur if artificial restrictions stood in the way of maximum efficiency.

There was something the ICC could do about the matter, and it did. In its governance arsenal was the service order. Declaring a war emergency, the ICC in September 1942 issued a service order instructing that carriers "operate their trains, when necessary for the prompt movement of freight, without regard to any rules, regulations, practices, or laws now in effect and being enforced in the various states."

For the duration of the war, there went the Arizona train-limit law. The brotherhoods didn't like the ruling at all, but they were overruled; the ICC's authority stood. Two related service orders, issued at the end of July 1943, were vacated six months later when the brotherhoods bowed to their terms.

However they came about, these service orders helped clear the way for the Santa Fe to begin making a far more modern railroad out of many of its lines. The full capabilities of the Santa Fe's new freight diesels could be put to work. In this regard, those in Santa Fe corner offices and wood-paneled boardrooms probably paused to give the government a nod of thanks.

Warbonnet FTs cruise past the construction site of a realignment project near Williams Junction, Arizona, in 1960. *Photo Santa Fe Railway, Wallace W. Abbey Collection*

TWELVE EIGHTY LOCOMOTIVES THE HARD WAY

Building the Fleet One EMD Order at a Time

IF IT HAD JUST BEEN A CASE OF SWITCHING FROM STEAM freight locomotives to diesels—no small switch, to be sure—the Santa Fe undoubtedly would have engineered a more orderly transition than it did. After all, it already had considerable experience with diesels, knew their advantages, and wanted to put them to greater use. Santa Fe ran through territories ready-made to show off diesels' attributes. Still, the railroad faced pressures from many directions—its own traditionalism, entrenched agreements with operating employees, long-standing state and federal laws, and a brewing war. We shouldn't be surprised that dieselizing its freight service took the Santa Fe's Mechanical Department and top management around many twists and turns.

While Santa Fe was Electro-Motive's best Model F customer, it was hardly its most organized. Between the end of 1940 and the late summer of 1945, the railroad acquired 320 units: 155 with cabs, 165 without. To build its fleet, Santa Fe presented Electro-Motive with 16 separate orders, for as many as 60 units and as few as one.

All 80 locomotives—that is, all 320 units—came from the factory decorated the same way. The main car body color was "Santa Fe blue," trimmed above and below in yellow. What some railfans would call the "postage stamp" treatment on the nose was also yellow. A square Santa Fe emblem, etched bronze on the earliest units and later painted, was the "stamp." A vermilion stripe separated the blue and yellow wherever the two colors met.

Locomotive number crunchers, keep one thing in mind: however road numbers of individual Model Fs, including the first factory order, might be redesignated, the original serial numbers never changed. No unit ever carried more than one factory serial number—a good thing for tracking purposes. Some units sported at least four different road numbers during their lifetime, while others carried their original numbers right to the scrap yard.

So here we go with a rundown of Santa Fe's FT orders after its first. There were few major differences in their specifications, except for improvements and modifications based on EMD's growing experience.

On February 19, 1941, with the 100 having been in service a little more than six weeks and the 101 not yet on the property, the Santa Fe placed with Electro-Motive an order for eight trailing or booster units, to be delivered in the fall.

When he first saw the Authority for Expenditure for the boosters, motive-power chief John Purcell instructed that it be rewritten to refer to two four-unit locomotives, not to eight individual units. Thereafter, billing documents and publicity referred to two 5,400-horsepower locomotives, even though there wasn't a cab in the bunch.

Facing, With FT diesels looming at an unidentified roundhouse in April 1945, a worker welds a bracket. *Photo Santa Fe Railway, Stan Kistler Collection*

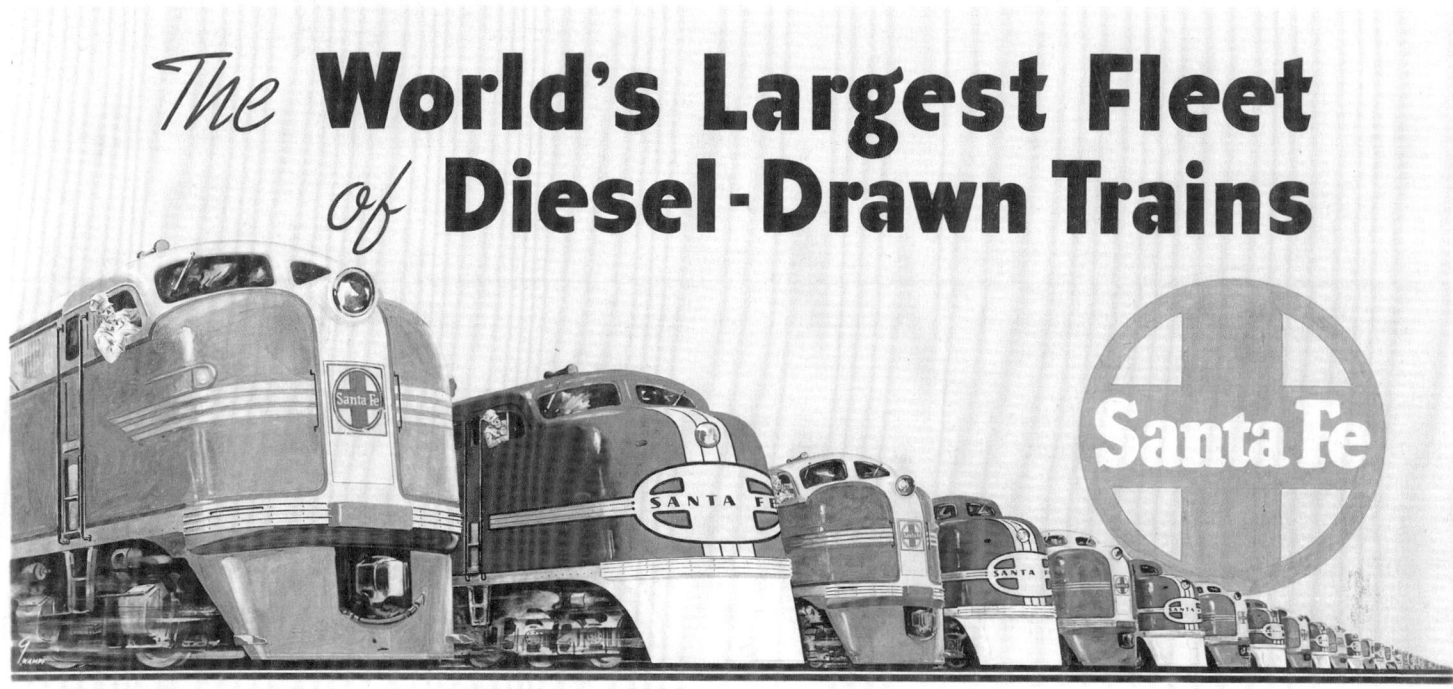

Facing, A window display, likely at Santa Fe headquarters in Chicago, touts the advantages of the new diesel fleet. *Photo Santa Fe Railway, Wallace W. Abbey Collection*

Above, Artwork for a highway billboard positions Santa Fe in the vanguard of the diesel revolution. *Photo Santa Fe Railway, Wallace W. Abbey Collection*

Promptly on their delivery to Shopton, the first two of the new boosters were substituted for the trailing cab units of the 100 and 101. Anticipating their service, the new boosters had been given road numbers 100C and 101C. The displaced cab units, with the same numbers, were sent back to Electro-Motive, regeared, and renumbered 102 and 103. On their return to Shopton, each was mated with three of the new boosters. Thus, before the end of September, the 100-class roster now consisted of four 5,400-horsepower locomotives, each with but one cab.

On March 25, 1941, Santa Fe placed two more orders. One was for a lead unit, the other for three boosters. The four units emerged from the EMD plant in November as the 104. That the locomotive came to the railroad by itself might be explained by upcoming design changes. Perhaps the 104 was built from components that were perfectly good but about to be superseded. Some of the mechanical and electrical details of the 105 were indeed different from its five predecessors.

The idea of 80-miles-per-hour diesel-powered freight trains evaporated. Beginning with the 105, all Model Fs, as individual units or as four-unit consists, were delivered as 65-miles-per-hour locomotives with 62:15 gear ratios. The earlier locomotives ultimately were modified to these specifications.

Sizable orders of four-unit locomotives with one lead unit each were ordered in May and December 1941 and April 1942.

Eighty Locomotives the Hard Way

With their delivery, Santa Fe's fleet had grown to 43 four-unit locomotives, running behind road numbers 100–142. To each set of booster units was appended the suffixes "A," "B," and "C."

The Santa Fe placed its largest order with Electro-Motive, 60 units, on June 26, 1942. Originally, the order specified 15 lead and 45 trailing units. Then, as the war effort heated up, the ICC loosened railroads' operating restrictions and the Santa Fe better maximized its rolling stock. Santa Fe changed its request, asking EMD to produce instead 33 lead units and 27 boosters.

The first three dozen units, delivered from EMD across the spring and summer of 1944, became nine four-unit locomotives, 143–151. There remained from this order 24 trailing units, delivered in October. Half would go to locomotives 120–131 as part of the continuing program of swapping new trailing units for cab units already in service; the other half was designated as a new set of two-cab, four-unit locomotives with the road numbers 152–157. From this point on, two cabs would be the standard on Santa Fe's four-unit locomotives.

Facing, The operator at West Winslow forks up train orders to the crew of FT 148, one of 60 units ordered from EMD in June 1942. *Photo Santa Fe Railway, Stan Kistler Collection*

Above, Carrying the white flags of an extra, FT 168, a member of the problematic 158 class of engines, leads a train through Cajon Pass. *Photo Joe G. Collias, Wallace W. Abbey Collection*

A 4-6-2 steam locomotive gives the three-unit diesel a hand on a freight heading south out of Chanute, Kansas. *Photo Wallace W. Abbey, Center for Railroad Photography & Art Collection*

FT diesels lead a westbound freight across Bridge 9-C over the Chicago Sanitary District canal east of McCook, Illinois. *Photo Wallace W. Abbey, Center for Railroad Photography & Art Collection*

Resplendent in latter-day blue-and-yellow paint, the 109 cruises over the Washita River bridge near Gene Autry, Oklahoma. *Photo Santa Fe Railway, kansasmemory.org, Kansas Historical Society*

Extra 199 West gets underway out of Argentine Yard in February 1953. In the distance, another westbound is ready to follow.
Photo Wallace W. Abbey, Trains *magazine, Kalmbach Media*

The noses of five other FTs poke out of roundhouse doors as the 116 rides the turntable at Winslow, Arizona, in 1945. *Photo Santa Fe Railway, Stan Kistler Collection*

Wearing Santa Fe's standard passenger paint scheme, the 167 leads an unidentified passenger train just west of the Illinois River bridge at Chillicothe. *Photo Wallace W. Abbey,* Trains *magazine, Kalmbach Media*

The 163, one of 10 FTs wired for passenger service and painted in Warbonnet livery, receives service at the 18th Street roundhouse in Chicago. *Photo Wallace W. Abbey, Center for Railroad Photography & Art Collection*

Passenger engine 15, an E6, shares track space at the 18th Street fueling rack with FT 160, September 2, 1946. *Photo Wallace W. Abbey, Center for Railroad Photography & Art Collection*

Above, The Alco PA diesel of the westbound *Grand Canyon Limited* picks up its FT helpers at Mojave, California, for the climb around Tehachapi Loop, April 1953. *Photo Wallace W. Abbey,* Trains *magazine, Kalmbach Media*

Facing, What the FT fleet begat: Santa Fe's new diesel shop at Barstow, California, shortly after its completion in 1948. *Photo Santa Fe Railway, Wallace W. Abbey Collection*

By now, the 100s were working mostly out of Winslow, which is where the unit swaps took place. When nothing but new lead units were delivered, Shopton would couple them together and send them west. The first groups of four went dead-in-tow. But then Shopton began to place the new units in revenue service on westbound trains, four at a time. The two middle units faced each other. Temporary jumper cables were run through their nose doors.

Over time, the original paint scheme of the FTs saw variations. Upon repainting, their vermilion accent stripes had a tendency to disappear. Some units temporarily showed up nearly all blue; before long, the yellow was back.

On May 24, 1943, EMD received its next order from the Santa Fe: 36 lead units. This order, delivered across the fourth quarter of 1944, also included the two lead and two trailing units of the 167.

The 167 wasn't the only FT used for passenger service; over time, 40 freight service FT units were temporarily rerigged to pull passenger trains. But the 167 was quite possibly the only Electro-Motive FT to be accorded the type "Special Freight." And thus, quite possibly, it was the only FT that had been specifically rigged for different duties, a passenger locomotive in freight service garb. Every axle beneath the 167 was powered to make it efficient and sure-footed. Its maximum permissible speed with its gear ratio of 57:20 was 95 miles per hour.

Its two trailing units each contained 3,000-cubic-foot-per-minute Vapor CFK-4225 steam generators. The 1,330-gallon tanks beneath its booster units held water for the steam generators, not fuel for the diesels. An additional 400 gallons of water were in tanks inside each car body, a feature that had been aboard the 103. Fuel for the engines in the trailing units came from the lead units' tanks.

Clearly, Model Fs could handle the heavier passenger trains. In early 1941, Electro-Motive's experimental 103 had conducted passenger-service tests, first pulling the *Ranger* between Chicago and Shopton. Then the 103 did six round trips between Chicago and Los Angeles leading the heavyweight *Fast Mail Express*, the *Grand Canyon Limited*, and the *California Limited*. The success of those tests had led the Southern Railway to purchase the 103.

Two more Model F orders from the Santa Fe awaited Electro-Motive. The first, in August 1944, requested 37 lead and 3 trailing units. They were delivered the following June. The lead-unit-for-trailing-unit swaps, completed in late 1944 for all locomotives newer than the 105, were completed for the first five 100s. Now, all road and serial numbers were in logical sequence.

The final FT order, eight units that would comprise the 178 and 179, was given to Electro-Motive in June 1945. Both locomotives were in service by early August, about a month before the end of World War II.

The 80-member freight diesel fleet as Santa Fe originally envisioned it was now together, except that for as long as they were in service the 100, 101, 102, 103, and 104 were composed of just one cab unit and three trailers. They didn't, however, always run in four-unit consists.

And those 40 locomotives that saw temporary duty pulling passenger trains? The units comprised the 158–166 and the 168. All incorporated the same electrical details as the 167 and each received its Warbonnet paint as it was converted. The locomotives, which became known as the 158 class, turned out to be roughriders. One of their chief benefits was to eliminate the need for passenger-service helpers.

In passenger service, however, the 158 class was not trouble-free. High speeds were incompatible with the FT's wheel and truck design, resulting in experiments with nonstandard wheels. The locomotive's length was incompatible with some passenger stations. These sorts of challenges helped push the FTs back into the freight business, where some in the 100 class were being reshuffled into three-unit sets.

All the 158-class locomotives were returned to freight service between May 1948 and December 1951. They were given back their freight locomotive specifications but not necessarily the paint scheme. The experience with long, heavy-duty locomotives in passenger service wasn't discarded when the FTs went back

AN ENDURING TRIBUTE TO FRED GURLEY

When Fred Gurley came to the Santa Fe in 1939 at age 50, he already had 33 years of railroading experience with the Chicago, Burlington & Quincy. He performed perhaps an outsized role in Santa Fe's management decisions. For two years he served as acting president while illness sidelined Ed Engel, then in 1944 he took the reins fully for 13 more. Gurley brought the railroad through the Depression and World War II and oversaw its efforts to regain a normal postwar footing. As the federal highway system began to mature and air travel ceased being a novelty, Gurley was challenged again and again to guide the future of the Santa Fe.

He led a 1948 celebration of the 100 millionth mile of diesel passenger service, cheered the beginning of daily schedules for the *Super Chief* and *El Capitan*, and lauded the railroad's diesel freight fleet. In between the festivities, Gurley often testified in seemingly endless labor disputes with union bosses.

Doubtless, involvement with Walt Disney was a pleasant diversion for Gurley. In 1954, the construction of Disneyland began on 139 acres of former orange groves in Anaheim, California. Running around the mile perimeter of the park, carrying happy guests, would be Walt's dream: a railroad. Disney's machine shop constructed 12 cars and, with help from outside frame and boiler manufacturers, 2 steam locomotives. To cut costs, Disney struck a sponsorship deal with Gurley. When it was finalized on March 29, 1955, the locomotives were dressed up with their new name: Santa Fe & Disneyland Railroad.

On July 17, 1955, Disneyland opened with appropriate fanfare. Walt Disney engineered steam locomotive No. 1 around the track, with Gurley and California governor Goodwin Knight in the cab. Celebrities Art Linkletter and Ronald Reagan joined in the fun. The No. 1, modeled after Central Pacific No. 173, was named *C. K. Holliday* in honor of Santa Fe's first president. Its companion, No. 2 *E. P. Ripley*, resembled Baltimore & Ohio No. 774 and paid tribute to the 14th Santa Fe president.

Fred Gurley. Trains *magazine, Kalmbach Media*

Within two years, the popularity of the Santa Fe & Disneyland Railroad convinced Walt he needed a third train. To reduce expenses, Disney wanted to refurbish an existing steam locomotive rather than build one from scratch. A search turned up an 0-4-4T built by the Baldwin Locomotive Works in August 1894, which had been used in a Louisiana sugarcane mill. After a $37,000 restoration that included conversion to a 2-4-4T, the No. 3 and a new batch of cars went into service at Disneyland on March 28, 1958.

Gurley, by then chair of the Santa Fe, must have been pretty pleased when he learned the name chosen for No. 3: *Fred Gurley*.

In 1974, Santa Fe's sponsorship ended and its name was dropped. The Disneyland Railroad has seen other changes, too, including the acquisition of two more Baldwin locomotives and in 2006–2007, the complete restoration of *Fred Gurley*, down to the last bolt. The list of new parts was long, headlined by a boiler, cab, water tender, driving wheels, and rear trucks.

Fred Gurley rolled back into service in March 2008, 50 years to the month from its inaugural run. The locomotive, today nearly 130 years old, brings joy to Disneyland's guests and pays tribute to a Santa Fe leader who both respected the diesel-electric and retained his love for steam.

At Cleburne, Texas, evidence of motive-power transition as an ancient 2-8-0 steam locomotive shares the shop floor with new F-unit diesels. *Photo Santa Fe Railway, Wallace W. Abbey Collection*

to pulling just freight trains. Newer locomotives of advanced designs were arriving, and some 158 steam generators found new homes.

———

After the Santa Fe's 179, Electro-Motive would deliver only 36 more Model Fs, 12 each to the Southern, the Great Northern, and the Rock Island. The last FT to roll off the line was a three-section set that went to the Rock Island on November 12, 1945—the end of an era.

———

Observers of the railroad mystique would later hold that Electro-Motive's Model F fomented a revolution in railroad motive power—that the FT changed railroading for the better and for all time. True? Was the FT, as *Trains* magazine's David P. Morgan put it, "the diesel that did it"?

Yes. To a point.

There's no doubt: All things considered, a suitable diesel could outperform a comparable steam locomotive to where, really, there was no contest. No other "other-than-steam" locomotive of this era seemed truly to be a competitor. No other manufacturer who might have wished to field a contender had the armory and the arsenal of General Motors, nor the head start. No locomotive builder other than GM had so aptly defined the ground it wanted to win.

Still, it's fair to suggest it wasn't a single diesel locomotive—the FT—but its family that deserves the term *ubiquitous* across freight railroading. Together, perhaps, the FT and its derivatives—the F2, F3, F5, F7, and F9—earn top honors. But neither can we overlook EMD's later GP7 and GP9 hood units, notable in their own rights.

Might it not be even more appropriate to nominate as "the diesel that did it" not any particular locomotive model but instead the prime mover, the Model 567 diesel engine, that thrummed inside all of them?

———

If so, what, then, was it the FT did?

Looking at freight railroading as a whole and over time, perhaps the FT's most significant contribution was that it broke the ice, and it widened many eyes. And it did much to keep the Santa Fe and other railroads fluid during World War II. Those were big and essential jobs. Somebody who'd been working a long time to find a way to do them had figured out how.

The 160 is ready for its first run west at the location of the author's summer job, Santa Fe's 21st Street shop in Chicago, April 20, 1946. *Photo Wallace W. Abbey, Center for Railroad Photography & Art Collection*

THIRTEEN A CLASS BY ITSELF

The Author's Retrospective

DURING WORLD WAR II, TOM HARLEY, CHIC KERRIGAN, AND Dave Wallace were inmates of Evanston Township High School north of Chicago, as was I. We were what would later become known as railfans, so intrigued by trains we'd almost suffer to see them in action.

Those were steam-locomotive days, of course, but our train-watching objective tended to be the new, colorful, elusive diesel-electrics. In due course, railroading became for us more than a spectator sport. We all found railroad jobs of one sort or another. In June 1944, in the Santa Fe Railway's diesel shop at 21st Street and Wentworth Avenue in Chicago, I hired out as a diesel repairman's helper.

The 21st Street shop was the first in US railroading to be built specifically for, and to be dedicated to, the care and feeding of diesel-electrics. It was the maintenance base for most of Santa Fe's passenger locomotives, a fleet then quite modest. Working 3:00 to 11:00 p.m., I'd open up crankcases for the mechanics, help bar over engines for air tests, pour steaming Crater compound into traction-motor gearboxes, help pull out cylinder heads and power assemblies, operate the traveling crane above the shop floor, and emulate the yard switchman when it was necessary to move locomotives around on the tracks.

The shop and its locomotives fascinated me. That fall, when I went back to high school, I'd ride a streetcar out Archer Avenue to the shop now and then to see what was going on. The Harley-Kerrigan-Wallace consortium and I kept up the tradition another nine months or so after I'd cleaned out my locker.

For all practical purposes, it was there at 21st Street—on a spring evening in 1945—that this book was born.

At the shop we talked with George McNeish, a diesel mechanic who had come in off the road. I had often been George's helper.

"You should have been here earlier," George said. "The *167* was in the shop."

We didn't understand. The *167*? A freight locomotive? From out west? What was it doing at 21st Street, a Dearborn Station satellite terminal nowhere near the freight yard? And what was it doing on an assignment routinely protected by red-nosed passenger units?

George shrugged. He knew only that earlier the *167*, a four-unit blue-and-yellow device of the freight service persuasion—geared for passenger train speeds, rigged with steam generators and an automatic train control system, an expensive necessity on the Illinois Division—had left the shop, backed down to Dearborn Station, and spirited the *Super Chief* away to California.

A freight diesel on the *Super Chief*? And we'd just missed it!

Now, if you, too, appreciated the exotic where locomotives were concerned, what would you have done? Why, of course, confirm its existence and, if at all possible, photograph it. I computed the schedule of that set of *Super Chief* equipment out to Los Angeles and back. On the day the *167* would show up again in Chicago, we would be unavailable for such mundane pursuits as school.

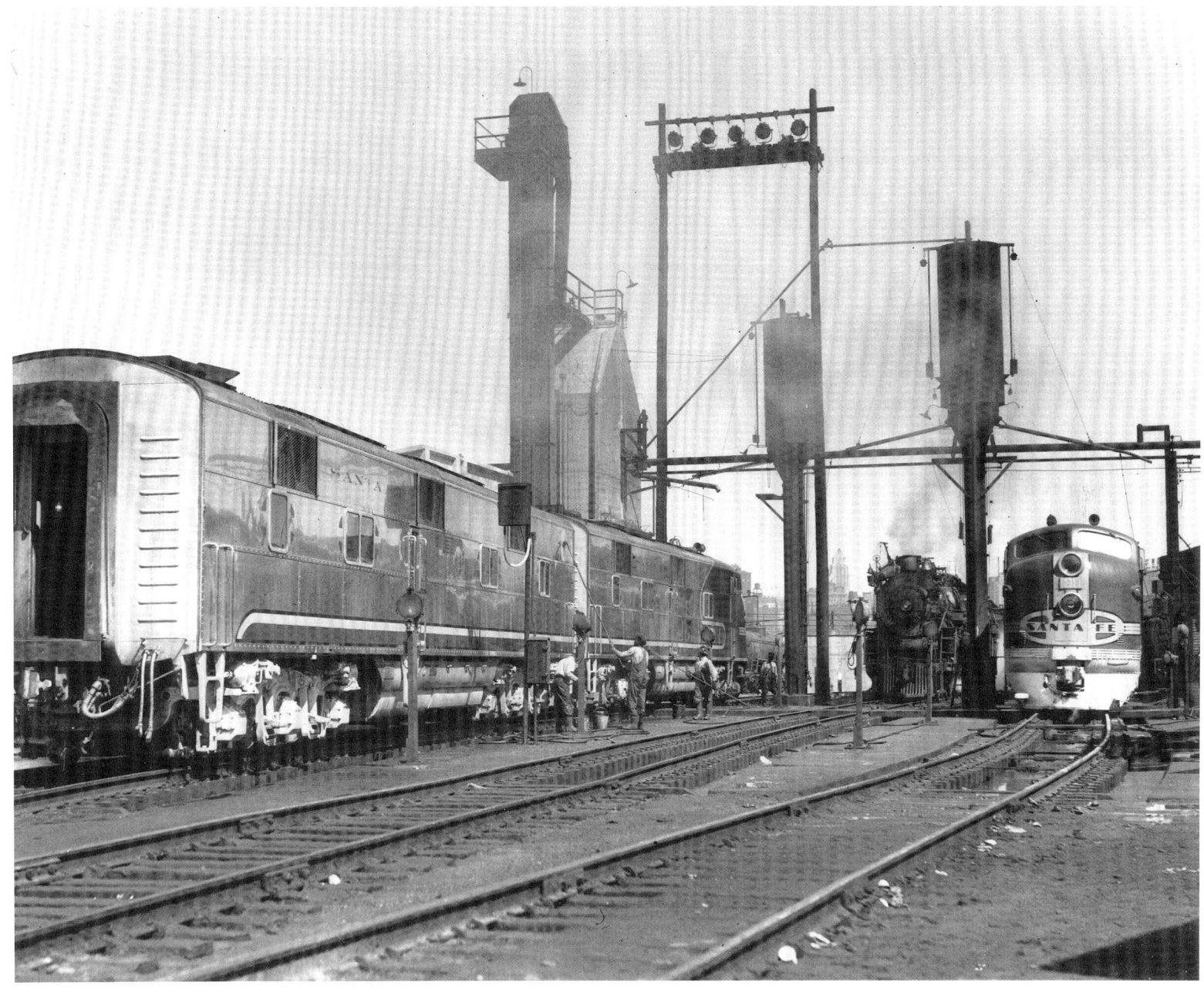

Facing, One of Abbey's best friends photographed the 100 heading eastbound through a familiar haunt, Willow Springs, Illinois. *Photo C. H. Kerrigan, Al Chione Collection*

Above, Steam and diesel mix at the 18th Street engine terminal, Chicago, on September 2, 1946. *Photo Wallace W. Abbey, Center for Railroad Photography & Art Collection*

Evanston was some distance from the Santa Fe, in fact from almost all Chicago's railroads. None of us had a car. But we were proficient in the use of public transportation and could get by train, streetcar, or bus to almost any point in the city, certainly to the spot we'd chosen for the appointed sighting.

We went from Central Street in Evanston down to North Western Station on Madison Street in downtown Chicago on a North Western "scoot"; then down Clinton Street on foot to Union Station; southwest on a Burlington suburban train to Harlem Avenue; south on a Chicago & West Towns bus to the railroad underpasses; up the embankment onto the Chicago & Illinois Western; and west along the C&IW track to a suitable location for a picture of a train on the Santa Fe, which ran parallel to it.

The day was chilly and damp. We arrived well ahead of when the *Super Chief* was due, aware that our odyssey might be in vain, that the 167 might have been diverted. So it was with considerable relief and excitement that we saw a train being led by a long blue-and-yellow diesel coming our way out of the west, shoving its headlight beam through the murk.

Out came the cameras.

Facing, The author encountered a pristine set of FTs in the red-and-silver Warbonnet paint at 21st Street, September 9, 1946. *Photo Wallace W. Abbey, Center for Railroad Photography & Art Collection*

Above, No. 100 leads train 40, called "the meat" for its heavy concentration of refrigerated cars for meat processors, through Coal City, Illinois, in 1945. *Photo Wallace W. Abbey, Center for Railroad Photography & Art Collection*

"It's a *freight* train!" We all identified it at the same instant: a train built largely of orange refrigerator cars and pulled by a locomotive with the road number 101.

A member of the 100 class—that is, a member other than the 167—had slipped its harness! It had wandered onto the easternmost reaches of the railroad to boot some laboring steam locomotive off its regular job. The type and class of locomotive that was bringing diesels to freight service for the first time, that we thought was out in Arizona and California helping to win the war, that we'd seen only in magazines and books—quite unexpectedly, one of those mystical machines had materialized out of the mist in McCook!

The *Super Chief* showed up not far behind the freight train, led, sure enough, by the 167. But that had become anticlimactic. We had seen another member of the 100 class, in its natural service but far from its natural habitat.

A Class by Itself

Shortly after its conversion for passenger service, the 160 hustles train 19, the *Chief*, near McCook, Illinois, on April 20, 1946. *Photo Wallace W. Abbey, Center for Railroad Photography & Art Collection*

While a college student, the author photographed the 175 hauling a westbound freight through the curves of Olathe Hill in Kansas, May 4, 1947. *Photo Wallace W. Abbey, Center for Railroad Photography & Art Collection*

Above, Running "left-handed," the 119 passes a classic Santa Fe signal bridge as it climbs up Olathe Hill, Kansas, with an eastbound freight. *Photo Wallace W. Abbey, Center for Railroad Photography & Art Collection*

Facing, An eastbound train passes through a new rock cut on the Ottawa Cutoff, part of a project to reduce curves between Zarah and Olathe, Kansas. *Photo Wallace W. Abbey, Center for Railroad Photography & Art Collection*

Above, While on assignment for *Trains* magazine, the author photographed oncoming Extra 186 East from the cab of westbound train 39 near Rock, Kansas. *Photo Wallace W. Abbey,* Trains *magazine, Kalmbach Media*

Facing, Descending into Ash Fork, Arizona, the Extra 235 West meets an eastbound train headed up the grade toward Supai Summit. *Photo Wallace W. Abbey,* Trains *magazine, Kalmbach Media*

I went back to 21st Street another day and watched from the shop door as a man in a suit and felt hat walked the 167 up from the roundhouse as if it were a Thoroughbred. With his kind permission, I climbed aboard and explored the 167's cabs and caverns.

On yet another day, I rode streetcars further out Archer Avenue to 38th Street and then west to Corwith Yard, at the time the Santa Fe's principal Chicago freight terminal. A member of the 100 class was at the roundhouse. It seemed awkwardly out of place in that ancient domicile of steam.

I asked around. Soon the story came together. The 167 was running in and out of Chicago regularly with passenger trains. The 100 and 101 were in freight service east of Argentine Yard in Kansas City. By fall, there would be five diesels in that service. Almost every day at about 2:00 p.m., a locomotive numbered 100, 101, 102, 103, or 104 would arrive at Corwith with No. 40, "the meat," the train we'd seen near McCook purely by happenstance. Promptly at 6:00 p.m., the diesel du jour would start back west with No. 39, the *Oklahoma-Texas Fast Freight*.

That fact-finding mission changed the pattern of my explorations of Chicago's railroads. I began to concentrate on those Santa Fe diesels for the balance of my high school days.

―――

That summer, 1945, I went to the University of Kansas (KU) at Lawrence. Frequently, the 167 would pause there with the *Kansas Cityan* passenger train or its equal and opposite *Chicagoan*. When the fall leaves came off the trees, from an upstairs window in Battenfeld Hall on Mount Oread, I could see the 167's flash of blue and yellow as it led the *Chicagoan* out of town.

South of Lawrence, on what was then called the Ottawa Cutoff, I discovered an occasional member of the 100 class among the 4-8-4s and related steam-breathing monsters that pulled the freight trains. The diesel would show up most regularly on No. 39. Hiking and hitchhiking, I'd scout out those 100s at Turner, Holliday, Zarah, on the curves of Olathe Hill in the Mill Creek Valley, and from my favorite place, the tower at Ottawa Junction.

Mid-April 1946, around suppertime and east of Lawrence, I photographed No. 11, the westbound *Kansas Cityan*, behind its customary red-nosed units. As I walked back toward town along the track, the westward automatic block signal ahead of me cleared up as 11 left the station, and then it dropped back. Its blade at 45 degrees told me that 11 had met an eastbound at the depot, although none was scheduled. Whatever train it was, it had come out of the passing track and was headed toward me, dumping the signals ahead of it. I could hear its air horn.

What soon appeared in the failing light was the 160, painted red and silver in its Warbonnet styling. It was running light—no train behind it, running extra—no timetable schedule. I would learn later it was on its way back to Argentine from Topeka, where it had been weighed after its conversion to a passenger-puller like the 167.

I went home to Illinois soon after and saw the 160 and photographed it again, this time as it led the *Chief* out of Chicago. Dieselization of transcontinental passenger trains other than the *Super Chief* and *El Capitan* had begun.

So started another pattern of exploration and photography: recording the use of locomotives built as freight-luggers on some of the nation's tonier passenger trains. With something of a vengeance, I pursued the 158 class through Illinois, Missouri, and Kansas.

―――

A freight train derailed at Edgerton, Kansas, on the Cutoff on August 31, 1948, splattering 32 cars over both main tracks and destroying the depot. By coincidence, I was aboard the eastbound *Oil Flyer* the next evening, coming back to KU via Kansas City. We crept through the house track to get around the pileup. The rather neatly accordion-pleated train was illuminated by the floodlights on the wrecking derrick. Until the derailment was picked up and the Cutoff reopened, 100s were in and out of Lawrence in quantity, detouring their trains between Holliday and Emporia over the First District. That was more freight than the First District perhaps had ever seen. And I had to be in class!

The locomotive on the train that had derailed, I learned later, was the Santa Fe's first of a new type and class of diesel: a successor to the 100s. Its road number was reported to me as 200.

―――

Facing, A clerk marks up engine assignments—including a number of FT diesels—on the massive train board at Cleburne, Texas. *Photo Wallace W. Abbey,* Trains *magazine, Kalmbach Media*

Above, The steam-to-diesel transition is in full force in this view at the Redondo Junction roundhouse in Los Angeles. *Photo Santa Fe Railway, Wallace W. Abbey Collection*

Facing, The 125 poses for its official portrait outside the EMD factory at La Grange. *Photo Electro-Motive Division, Wallace W. Abbey Collection*

Unless it was doing a predelivery break-in trip, that might not have been so; the 200, an F3, wouldn't be sold to the Santa Fe by EMD for two more months. Still, F3s and F7s and more versatile machines known as road switchers soon would set the 100s to wandering widely in search of a second glorious history.

Such a glory couldn't be found. Too much had changed. Though freight traffic was still high, by 1948 the war was over and new motive power was on the scene. The 100s were no longer as essential as they had been. There were no battles to fight with altitude, grade, tonnage, traffic volume, and bad or no water that couldn't be fought better by newer locomotives.

By then, too, railway labor organizations were settling into the inevitability of diesels in freight service and to the reality of job reductions compared to the days of steam. The newer road switchers were changing the operating landscape of not just the Santa Fe but the entire railroad industry.

And the Santa Fe's 100s? They were weary and wearing out. Their lasting value would be as progenitors of a freight-moving diesel fleet that was growing rapidly in diversity, size, technology, and power.

—⁂—

Ultimately, railroads in my life moved from hobby to career. As reporter and editor, I encountered the 100s in Illinois, Missouri, Kansas, New Mexico, and Texas. I saw them operating singly on locals and assembled in threes, fours, and fives on the main line.

As a fleet, the 100-class FTs were gone from the Coast Lines before I made it out to Arizona and California, to where those pioneers had performed their legendary service during the war. On a trip for *Trains* magazine in 1953, I inspected the long, steep struggle from Winslow up to the Arizona Divide at Riordan and the tortuous ride back down to Seligman. I did so over the snout of a 6,000-horsepower successor to the 100s, F7 No. 235. West of Winslow, the Santa Fe was infamous for its long uphill grades and therefore a great place to employ a graceful way to get a train down the mountain. How best to do that had been introduced to all diesel railroading by the 100s. On the descent from Supai through the Johnson Canyon Tunnel, I saw how a whining device called the dynamic brake could hold in check all that tonnage the 235 had booted up the hill.

And how things change! Soon, much of that territory would be bypassed by a new line on a much more forgiving grade.

I saw on this trip a railroad greatly improved since the war years. Soon, Santa Fe would eliminate the last steam locomotive from regular service, a final nod to the 100s that had shoved steam power out to pasture and to scrap.

—⁂—

In due course the 100s, too, would be destroyed, in small part by the economics of refunding to their manufacturer parts usable in newer and better locomotives, in far larger part by time and technology. The last of the Santa Fe's 320 FT units was retired in 1966. By chance I saw its obituary in a railfan publication. The credit for its residual value had been applied to the purchase of a locomotive that couldn't use many of its parts: a 3,600-horsepower hood unit called the SD45.

In that quarter century, diesel-electric locomotives had changed radically, inside and outside both. The horsepower per unit of the freight-moving devices constructed by Electro-Motive had doubled, and even greater increases were in prospect. Save for their basic concepts, the successors that ended the story of the 100 class were very much a new breed compared with the diesels that had stormed Cajon, conquered Tehachapi, and flattened the Arizona Divide at the time of World War II.

So be it. If it weren't for progress in dieselization as elsewhere in railroading, there might be no railroads for us to rely on and to enjoy.

—⁂—

Still, sounding quite like a railfan, I want to declare that if there's an all-time classic diesel-electric locomotive, it was the Santa Fe's 100-class FT.

The FTs on the Santa Fe started three revolutions: one in the diesel-electric locomotive itself; another in the properties over which the locomotives ran; and a third in how the skills of the people who managed and operated them were applied. With few complaints about their working conditions, those pioneer 100s dug in and pulled a world of freight as they pulled past a world of tradition.

By any measure you care to apply, this class of locomotives was a class by itself.

In repose: FT 189 is parked with cabooses at Santa Fe's Corwith Yard in Chicago. *Photo Wallace W. Abbey,* Trains *magazine, Kalmbach Media*

BIBLIOGRAPHY

The material in this book is taken from two broad sources: published works and unpublished works. The editors have, to the extent possible, reconstructed the bibliography of the author and apologize for omissions or errors.

Published Works: Articles, Books, Newsletters, Pamphlets, Reports

Armitage, Merle. *Homage to the Santa Fe: The Many Facets of Big Time Railroading*. El Cajon, CA: Manzanita, 1973.

———. *Operations Santa Fe: Atchison, Topeka & Santa Fe System*. New York: Duell, Sloan and Pearce, 1948.

Atchison, Topeka and Santa Fe Railway Co. *Annual Reports for the Years Ending Dec. 31, 1939, 1940, 1941*. Topeka, KS: Atchison, Topeka and Santa Fe Railway.

Barriger, John Walker, IV. *The Development of the Santa Fe, 1935–1948*. Thesis, Department of Business and Engineering Administration. Cambridge, MA: Massachusetts Institute of Technology Press, 1949.

Berkman, Pamela, ed. *The History of the Atchison, Topeka & Santa Fe*, Great Rails Series. New York: Smithmark, 1996.

Broggie, Michael. *Walt Disney's Railroad Story: The Small-Scale Fascination That Led to a Full-Scale Kingdom*. Pasadena, CA: Pentrex Media Group, 1997.

Bryant, Keith L. *History of the Atchison, Topeka and Santa Fe Railway*. New York: Macmillan, 1974.

Decades of the Diesel. Detroit, MI: General Motors, 1964.

Duke, Donald, and Stan Kistler. *Santa Fe: Steel Rails Through California*. San Marino, CA: Golden West, 1963.

83,000 Miles: The Story Behind the Diesel Freight Locomotive. La Grange, IL: Electro-Motive, 1941.

Ellington, Frank M. *Steam Locomotives of the Santa Fe: A Former Shopman's Scrapbook*. Panora, IA: Railroad Car, 1989.

Farrington, S. Kip. *Railroading from the Head End*. New York: Doubleday, Doran & Company, 1943.

Hutchinson [Kansas] News-Herald. Various articles, April 1941.

"Indians Dub Santa Fe's New Engine 'Lightning Wagon.'" *Gallup [New Mexico] Independent*, February 2, 1941.

Jones, Harry E. *Railroad Wages and Labor Relations, 1900–1952: An Historical Survey and Summary of Results*, 1953. Whitefish, MT: Literary Licensing, Reprint 2012.

Kettering, Eugene W. *History and Development of the 567 Series of General Motors Locomotive Engine*. La Grange, IL: Electro-Motive Division, 1951.

Kirkland, John F. *Dawn of the Diesel Age: The History of the Diesel Locomotive in America*. Glendale, CA: Interurban, 1983.

———. *The Diesel Builders, Vol. 3: Baldwin Locomotive Works*. Glendale, CA: Interurban, 1994.

Levinson, Harold L., C. M. Rehmus, J. P. Goldberg, and M. L. Kahn. *Collective Bargaining and Technological Change in American Transportation*. Evanston, IL: Northwestern University, 1981.

McCall, John B. *Santa Fe's Early Diesel Daze, 1935–1953*. Dallas, TX: Kachina, 1980.

Mirkin, Stanford M. *What Happened When: A Noted Researcher's Almanac of Yesterdays*. New York: Ives Washburn, 1966.

National Railway Bulletins 53-1, 1988, and 63-6, 1998. National Railway Historical Society.

Nelson, Donald. *Arsenal of Democracy: The Story of American War Production*. San Diego, CA: Harcourt, 1946.

Poling-Kempes, Leslie. *The Harvey Girls: Women Who Opened the West*. New York: Marlowe & Company, 1991.

Railfan & Railroad Magazine. Various articles, 1985, 1986, 1989. New York: Carstens.

Railroad Magazine. Various articles, 1944, 1956, 1957. New York: Popular.

Railway Age. Various articles, 1935–1945. Chicago: Simmons-Boardman.

Railway Signaling, August 1948. Chicago: Simmons-Boardman.

R&LHS Bulletin No. 75. New York: Railway & Locomotive Historical Society, January 1949.

Reck, Franklin M. *The Dilworth Story: The Biography of Richard Dilworth, Pioneer Developer of the Diesel Locomotive.* New York: McGraw Hill, 1954.

———. *On Time: The History of Electro-Motive Division of General Motors Corporation.* La Grange, IL: Electro-Motive Division, 1948.

Repp, Stan. *The Super Chief: Train of the Stars.* San Marino, CA: Golden West, 1980.

Rose, Joseph R. *American Wartime Transportation.* Springfield, OH: Crowell-Collier, 1953.

The Santa Fe Magazine. Various articles. Topeka, KS: Atchison, Topeka and Santa Fe Railway, 1941 to 1949.

"Streamlined Freight Here Friday." *Gallup [New Mexico] Independent*, February 7, 1941.

Thomas, Hadley A. *Any Other Country Except My Own.* Notre Dame, IN: Cross Cultural, 1994.

Trains. Various articles, 1941, 1946, 1948, 1949, 1962, 1965, 1966. Milwaukee, WI: Kalmbach.

Trains staff, eds. *Our GM Scrapbook.* Milwaukee, WI: Kalmbach, 1971.

Wikipedia. "Charles F. Kettering." Accessed September 23, 2020. https://en.wikipedia.org/wiki/Charles_F._Kettering.

———. "Edward Payson Ripley." Accessed September 23, 2020. http://en.wikipedia.org/wiki/Edward_Payson_Ripley.

———. "Fred Gurley." Accessed September 24, 2020. https://en.wikipedia.org/wiki/Fred_Gurley.

———. "Rudolf Diesel." Accessed September 23, 2020. https://en.wikipedia.org/wiki/Rudolf_Diesel.

———. "Samuel M. Vauclain." Accessed September 20, 2020. https://en.wikipedia.org/wiki/Samuel_M._Vauclain.

Winslow [Arizona] Mail. Various articles, 1940 to 1945.

Worley, E. D. *Iron Horses of the Santa Fe Trail: A Definitive History, in Fact and Photograph, of the Motive Power of One of America's Great Railroads.* Southwest Railroad Historical Society, 1965.

Wright, Roy V. *Locomotive Cyclopedia, 1941 Edition.* Milwaukee, WI: Kalmbach, Facsimile Reprint, 1971.

Zimmermann, Karl R. *Santa Fe Streamliners: The Chiefs and Their Tribesmen.* New York: Quadrant, 1987.

Unpublished Works

Atchison, Topeka and Santa Fe Railway. Corporate materials including board of directors minutes, various meetings, 1932–1947; advertising and promotion; correspondence; documents, news releases; papers; speeches; testimony, 1930–1995. Topeka, KS.

———. Engineering Department studies and track charts, 1941–1992.

———. Mechanical Department blueprints, diagrams, drawings, locomotive studies, 1941–1997.

———. Operating Department rule books, train sheets, timetables, 1941–1964.

———. Test Department locomotive studies and test reports, 1920–1953.

Electro-Motive Division, General Motors Corp. Corporate materials including advertising and publicity, correspondence, diagrams, internal documents, papers, speeches, testimony, 1939–1968. La Grange, IL.

———. Engineering Department central files, correspondence, instruction manuals, internal documents, locomotive materials, maintenance manuals, 1939–1988.

John W. Barriger III National Railroad Library, Special Collections. Various documents. St. Louis Mercantile Library at University of Missouri, St. Louis.

Kansas Historical Society. Various documents. Topeka, KS.

Minnesota Historical Society. Various documents. St. Paul, MN.

Scholz, Richard. Document Collection, 1870–1990. Santa Fe Railway Historical and Modeling Society. San Bernardino, CA.

Stagner, Lloyd E. Santa Fe Railway Collection. Harvey County Historical Society. Newton, KS.

United States Government. Various documents and testimonies from National Labor Relations Board, 1939–1944; National Railroad Adjustment Board, 1966; Office of Defense Transportation, 1943–1945; Reconstruction Finance Corporation, 1942–1954; War Production Board, 1941–1947. Washington, DC: Library of Congress.

United States Patent and Trademark Office. Various documents, 1937–1942. Washington, DC.

The author also acknowledges those with whom he had correspondence and interviews. These railroaders include Robert Aldag, John A. Angold, Larry Brashear, Fred Burchett, Henry Chastain, John Cline, Preston Cook, Major Timothy J. Cowan, John C. Davis, Robert L. Dixon, Fred W. Frailey, Milton H. Gardner, William A. Gardner, John G. German, Hugh Greer, Thomas E. Harley, Phillips C. Kauke, Stan Kistler, Paul E. LaCosse, Robert E. Lowrie, Joe McMillan, John Morris, Brian Moseley, Howard Neitzert, John Shedd Reed, Ted Rose, Francis E. Stuppi, John J. Wheelihan, and Glenn Young.

INDEX

Locators in italics indicate photographs.

Abbey, Wallace W., vii–x, 187
Abo Canyon, *44*, 104
Adams & Westlake, 126
Allis-Chalmers, 79
American Locomotive Company, 46, 54, 147; box-cab 1000, 57, *58*
Amtrak, 12
Arizona crew law, 158
Arizona Divide, 46, 104, *105*, *153*, 202
Arizona train-length law, 46, 158, 164
Atchison, Topeka & Santa Fe. *See* Santa Fe Railway

B&O Railroad Museum, 57
Baldwin Locomotive Works, 36, 38, 40, 46, 49; No. 58501 freight diesel, 54, *55*, 57
Baltimore & Ohio Chicago Terminal, 79, 93
Baltimore & Ohio Railroad, E-series units, 68
Barriger, John W., III, 114
Bessemer Gas Engine Company, 57
Bethlehem Steel, 51
Blomberg, Martin, 75
Boston & Maine Railroad, 57; *Flying Yankee*, 65
Brotherhood of Locomotive Engineers, 153, 154, 157
Brotherhood of Locomotive Firemen & Engineers, 153, 154, 156–157
Brotherhood of Railroad Trainmen, 153
Budd, Ralph, 63

Burlington Northern Santa Fe, 4
Burlington *Zephyrs*, 52, 63, 65, *67*, 121, 134

Cajon Pass, *28*, *39*, 106, *137*, *162*, 202; Sullivan's Curve, *16*, 140
California tonnage law, 46, 158
Canadian National Railway, 54, 57, 96
Canadian Pacific Railway, 96
Canyon Diablo, *14*, 46
Caterpillar. *See* Progress Rail
Central Railroad of New Jersey, 57; box-cab 1000, *58*
Century of Progress World's Fair, 63, 65
Cherryvale, Kansas, viii, 35
Chesapeake & Ohio Railway, 96
Chicago, Burlington & Quincy Railroad, 5, 18, 62, 63, 75, 92, 121, 190; S-4 steam locomotive, 68. *See also* Burlington *Zephyrs*
Chicago, Rock Island & Pacific Railroad, 96, 185; TA diesel, 88
Chicago & Eastern Illinois, 4; *Dixie Flagler*, 7
Chicago & Illinois Western, 190
Chicago & North Western Railway, viii
Chicago & Western Indiana, 4
Chicago Great Western Railroad, 54
Chicago Union Station, 67, 190
Communications methods, 30–31, 108
Cravens, Claude, 104, 108

Dayton Engineering Laboratories Company (Delco), 52, 73, 79
De La Vergne Refrigerating Machine Company, 52
Dearborn Station, Chicago: 4, *7*, *8*, *21*, 35, *69*, 130, 187
Diesel, Rudolf, 45, 52, 54, 55
Diesel-electric motive power, vii, 3, 54, 90, 202
Diesel Power magazine, 134, 140
Diesel prime mover, 12, 57, 65, 70, 75, 77, 90
Dilworth, Richard M., 54, 63, 68, 75, 96, *98*, *128*, 143; Presidential Emergency Board testimony, 90, 93, 154–155
Disney, Walt, 183
Doubleheader rule, 158

Electro-Motive Corporation, 3, 51–54, 57, 61, 63, 75, 77, 126, 145; acquired by General Motors, 61; Cleveland office, 53; conception of freight diesel, 77; E unit 511 and 512 demonstrators, *67*, 68, 77, 79; E unit *Streamliners*, 75, 77, 89; Electro-Motive Engineering Corporation, 51; Engineering Department, 123; E6 demonstrator, *9*; La Grange factory, vii, *64*, *66*, 68, 73, 75, *76*, 77, 79, *81*, 110, 119, 123, 130, 140, 143, *201*; Model 60 box-cabs, 61; Navy Building at La Grange, 147; switchers, 66. *See also* FT 103 demonstrator *and* Model 567 engine

207

Electro-Motive Diesel, 3
Electro-Motive Division, vii, 3, 51, 62, 77; La Grange factory expansion, 68; Navy Building at La Grange, 151; Santa Fe FT orders, 167; supplies navy, 143, 145–147, 151
Engel, Edward J., 114, 121
Erie Railroad, 4
Evanston, Illinois, vii, viii, 187, 190

Fairbanks-Morse, 54, 96, 143, 147
Florida East Coast Railway, 96
Fowler, Volney B., 130
Fred Harvey service, 4, 5, 17, 18
Freeman, Lewis D., 114, 116–117
FT 103 demonstration tour, 94; *83,000 Miles* book, 94; employee reaction, 100, 153; on non-Santa Fe properties, *87, 88,* 94, 110, *118*; on the Santa Fe, 94, 97–110; Santa Fe recommendations, 119; test report summary, 113–114, 116–117
FT 103 demonstrator, 76, 77, *107, 125*; assembly, 81–86; Blomberg truck, *83*; brake systems, *82*, 113–114, 140; cab controls, 100, *102–103*; cab layout, *85*; control stand, *161*; comparison to Santa Fe 100s, 124, 126; comparison to steam, 94, 113; completed at La Grange, 93; cooling system, 89; design rationale, 90, 93; dynamometer car, *87,* 100, 103, *115*; final orders, 185; first appearance, 93; gear ratio, 82, 84; horsepower, 84, 116; labor implications, 89, 158; paint scheme, 88; road numbers, 88; sold to Southern Railway, *91,* 94; steam generator, *82*; traction motors, 82; welded underframes, 72–73. *See also* Model F (or FT) freight diesel *and* Model F Standard

Gardner, Milton, 77, 79
Gardner-Denver, 79
General Electric, 52, 54, 68, 79; box-cab 1000, *57, 58*
General Motors Corporation, 3, 52, 61–62, 66, 79; acquires Electro-Motive, 61; acquires Winton, 61; Cleveland Diesel Division, 62, 147; Detroit Diesel, 145; Electro-Motive Division, 62; Fisher Body, 145; Research Labs, 143; success of FTs, 185; supplies US Navy, 143
Golden Glow headlight, 36
Grand Trunk Western, 4
Great Northern Railway, 96, 185
Gulf, Colorado & Santa Fe, 32
Gurley, Fred, 49, 104, 121, 164; involvement with Disney, 183

Hamilton, Harold L., 51, 52, 54, 61, *63*, 75, 77; War Production Board, 145
Hannibal & St. Joseph Railroad, 18
Harley, Tom, 187
Harrison, 79
Harvey, Fred, 18
Hinckley and Pittsburgh Works, 38
Hooven, Owens, Rentschler Company, 54

Illinois Central Railroad, 96
Indiana Harbor Belt, 66
Ingersoll-Rand, 54; box-cab 1000, *57, 58*
Internal-combustion engine, 45, 52, 54, 61
Interstate Commerce Commission, 19, 25, 164, 170

J. G. Brill, 51

Kansas City Southern, 75
Kansas City Union Station, 36
Kerrigan, Chic, 187, 189
Kettering, Charles F., *50,* 52, 61, *63*
Kettering, Eugene, 63, 65
Klein, Chris J., 75
Knickerbocker, Leland, 75

Labor unions, 88, 89, 90, 126, 153–157, 164
Lackawanna Railroad, 96
Lautz, H. B., 99
Lemp, Hermann, 54
London, Midland & Scottish, 54
Luken Steel, 72
Lyles, Lee, 130, 134

McIntosh & Seymour, 54
McKeen Company, 52, 54, 57
McNeish, George, 187

Milwaukee Road, 5; F7 steam locomotive, 68
Minneapolis, St. Paul, Rochester & Dubuque Electric Company, "Dan Patch" line, 54, *56*
Minneapolis & St. Louis Railway, 96
Minnesota Transportation Museum, 54
Model F (or FT) freight diesel, vii, viii, 3, 4, 51, *120, 123,* 185; final orders, 185; FT-SB, 96; independent units vs. dependent sections, 89, 96, 116, 124, 126, 158; industry holdouts, 96; initial Santa Fe interest, 93; on non-Santa Fe properties, 3, 96, 185; successors to, 96, 151, 202; total production, 96. *See also* Santa Fe 100-class FTs
Model F Standard, 76, 77, 79, 82, 84, 88–90, 93–94, 124; compared to *Streamliners*, 89; economics, 90; engineering release, 79, 123–124; Freight Thirteen, 3, 79; horsepower, 77, 79, 84, 96, 154–155, 158; multiple control, 90; volume production, 90, 96. *See also* FT 103 demonstrator
Model 567 engine, 65, 68, *70, 71,* 72, 75, 77, 89, 185; in navy use, *142,* 143, 146–147; variations of, 68, 72
Model 184 engine, in navy use, 65, 143, 145–147
Model 201 engine, 62, 65, 66
Model 201A engine, 65, 68, 77; in navy use, 143, 145, 146
Monon Railroad, 4
Morgan, David P., vii, 185
Morris, John, *98, 128,* 140

National Cash Register, 52
New York, New Haven & Hartford Railroad, 96
New York Central, J-1 steam locomotive, 68
Nickel Plate Road, 96
Norfolk & Western Railway, 96
North Western Station, 190
Northern Pacific Railroad, 3, 54

Olathe Hill, *34, 193, 194,* 199
Order of Railway Conductors, 153
Osgood-Bradley, 51
Ottawa Cutoff, *195,* 199
Otter, William D., 75

Pacific Railway Club, 77, 145
Panama-Pacific International Exposition, 40, 43
Panhandle & Santa Fe Railroad, 32
Patton Motor Company, 52
Pennsylvania Railroad, 5, 54, 57, 96
Player, John, 38
Presidential Emergency Board, First Diesel Case, 90, 94, 154–155, 157
Progress Rail, 3
Pullman Company, 30, 52
Pullman Standard, 51
Purcell, John, 40, 99, 102, *130*, 167

Raton Pass, *41*
Reading Company, 54
Reed, John Shedd, 100
Ripley, Edward, 5
Roosevelt, Franklin D., 15, 157

St. Louis Car Company, 51, 61, 68
Sanders, E. G., 99
Santa Fe diesel locomotives and trains, "Amos 'n Andy," 52, 79; *Chief*, 4, *16*, *192*, 199; E units 1A and 1B, *21*, 68, 69, 72, 75; *El Capitan*, 4, *7*, *20*, 75, *107*, 199; E1 diesels *74*, *75*; *Grand Canyon Limited*, 33, 35, 42, 110, *180*, 182; M.184 "doodlebug," *59*; M.190 "doodlebug," *61*, *62*; *Super Chief*, 4, 6, 9, 13, 31–33, *62*, 73, 75, *107*, *187*, *190*–191, 199; Warbonnet paint scheme, 73, *74*, *174*, *178*, *190*, 199. *See also* Santa Fe 100-class FTs
Santa Fe dieselization, 12, 100, 134, *167*, *184*, 200, 202; freight, 4, 11, 15, 47–48, 122; passenger, 30, 182; switching, 30, 66, 202
Santa Fe facilities, Argentine Yard, 22, 99, 103, 104, 108, 109, 134, 135, *175*, 199; Barstow diesel shop, 107–108, 134, *181*; Clovis yard, 99, 104, 108–110, *111*, 134; Corwith Yard, 99, 103, 104, 108–110, 199, *203*; 18th Street shops, 2, 130, *178*, *179*, *189*; Emporia yard, 99, 104, 108, 134; Redondo Junction roundhouse, *200*; San Bernardino shops, 47, 103, 106–108; Shopton, 109, 126, *129*, 134, 140, *141*, 169, 182; Topeka shops, 99, 103, 104, 199; 21st Street shops, 27, *186*, *187*, *190*, 199; Wellington, 24, 99, 108, 134; West Wichita Shops, 108
Santa Fe 100-class FTs, 167–182, 185, 202; cab and trailing unit swaps, 169, 170, 182; employee reaction, 100; first order, 123, 124, 126; labor implications, 126, 153, 156–157; last order, 182; last retired, 202; No. 100 preview, 126, *127*; No. 100 public tour, *128*, *129*, 130–140; Nos. 100–103, 167, 169, 182; No. 104, 167; Nos. 100–142, 170; No. 105, 169; Nos. 143–151, 170; Nos. 152–157, 170; Nos. 158–166 and No. 168 (158 class), 182, 185; No. 167 (Special Freight), 182; Nos. 178–179, 182; paint scheme, 167, 182; serial and road numbers, 126, 140, 167; speeds, 121, 123, 169
Santa Fe Railway, 3–15, 17, 93; authorization of first FT, 121, 123; car fleet, 30; company image, 17; divisions, 32; Fred Harvey relationship, 18; grades, 31; John Shedd Reed essay, 100; labor relations, 158; management structure, 32; Mechanical Department, 93, 124, 167; 1939 annual report, 25; Test Department, 100, 123, 124, 130; track, 30; truck lines, 25; wartime traffic, 151
Santa Fe steam locomotives, 35–49, 134; amortization of, 49; "Blue Goose" 4-6-4, *74*; comparison to diesels, 49; compounding, 38–39, *40*, 43, 46; decline of, 49; fleet, 29, 35–49; 4-6-2 No. 3600, 40, 43; single-expansion articulateds, 46; 2-10-2 Santa Fe wheel type, 39
Schenectady Locomotive Works, 38
Seaboard Air Line, E unit 822, 75, 79; E units 3000 and 3001, 79, *80*
Sloan, Alfred, 61
Southern Pacific Railroad, 51, 57, 96, 185
Southern Railway 6100, *91*, 94
Standard Steel Car, 51
Storey, William, 5
Sulzer Brothers Machine Works, 45, 54

Taunton Locomotive Works, 38
Texas & Pacific Railway, 96
Topeka Daily Capital newspaper, 131
Trains magazine, vii, 185, 202
Turner, Paul, 51

Union Pacific Railroad, 96; *M10000* streamliner, 52, *60*; single-expansion articulateds, 46
United Fruit Company, 61
University of Kansas, viii, 35, 199
US Supreme Court, 158

Vauclain, Samuel, 55
Von Linde, Carl, 45

Wabash Railroad, 4, 96
Wallace, Dave, 187
White Motor Company, 51
William Beardmore Company, 54, 57
Winslow Mail newspaper, 114
Winton Engine Company, 51, 54, 57, 51, 61, 65, 66; acquired by General Motors, 61
Woodward, 79
World War I, 5, 30, 47, 54, 145
World War II, beginning of, 143; build up to, 3, 15; railroading during, 3, 18, 30, 35, 46, 49, 143, 148–151, 164, 170, 185; US Army, *149*, 151; US Navy, 65, 142, 147, *150*, 151; War Production Board, 145

Index

Wallace W. Abbey (1927–2014) spent his career as a railroad journalist and public-relations executive, primarily in the Upper Midwest. His combined writing and photographic skills documented well the dynamic railroad landscape from the 1940s through the 1980s. Although Wally never worked for the Santa Fe, it was his favorite railroad, in part because of its 100-class diesel-electrics.

Kevin P. Keefe is a Milwaukee-based journalist, former editor and publisher of *Trains* magazine, and author of *Twelve Twenty-five: The Life and Times of a Steam Locomotive*, winner of a 2017 Notable Book Award from the Library of Michigan. Kevin continues to write for railroad publications and is also a member of the board of directors of the Center for Railroad Photography & Art.

Martha Abbey Miller inherited from her father, Wally Abbey, a love of both railroads and the written word. Following a career in communications management for technology companies including Hewlett-Packard, she is a writer, editor, and author of several nonfiction books. Martha is a member of the boards of directors of Haiti Education Foundation and Haiti Healthcare Partners. She lives in Prescott, Arizona.